Growing Vegetables 1001 Questions Answered

ADRIENNE and PETER OLDALE

SPHERE BOOKS LIMITED
30/32 Gray's Inn Road London, WC1X 8JL

First published in Great Britain by David & Charles Ltd
1976
Copyright © Adrienne and Peter Oldale 1976
Published by Sphere Books 1977

Set in Intertype Baskerville

Printed in Great Britain by
Hunt Barnard Printing Ltd
Aylesbury, Bucks

Digging for survival is fast becoming a national pastime. Over eighty per cent of the population of Britain lives in towns – making us, statistically, the most urban people in the world – but more and more people are today aware of the pleasures and profits to be gained from producing their own food instead of relying on the local greengrocer or supermarket. In the last year alone, the demand for allotments has more than doubled as townspeople have worked out that growing vegetables not only stretches the housekeeping budget but also provides fresher, more nutritious and flavoursome foods, frequently leading to more tasty and imaginative dishes, not forgetting the unique satisfaction to be gained from shaking the earth off potatoes which they personally have sown, tended and dug.

In the following pages, the first-time gardener will find all the information he needs on how to go about making the most of his vegetable patch. Part 1 gets right down to basics with the raw materials of gardening: what kind of soil? when to feed it? how much water? which fertilizers? Simple sub-divisions and the question-and-answer format ensure that the book is easy to use, whatever your current interest, be it making compost, types of manure or crop rotation. Within each section, questions progress from a simple starting point, building up a comprehensive overall picture, including detailed replies of interest to the more experienced vegetable grower.

Part 2 comes to grips with exactly what to grow, when and how, from artichokes to watercress. There is substantial coverage of the standard garden vegetables, but the more unusual also have a place: celeriac, chou de burghley, couve trouchuda, endive, scorzonera – all can be grown in English soil, and there are even hints on how to cook them. Taken in alphabetical order, each vegetable is dealt with logically, from planting and cultivation, through dealing with likely pests and diseases, to harvesting and storage. The essentially practical suggestions such as the best way to stop tomatoes splitting when they ripen, alternative salad vegetables to grow in cold areas, how to stop spinach and lettuce from 'bolting', are complemented by unusual details known only to experienced growers. Did you know, for instance, that you can graft a tomato onto a potato to produce a 'tomato' with potatoes on the roots and tomatoes on the shoots?

Growing vegetables need not be a full-time job. It has been estimated that, to be completely self-sufficient, we would each need to cultivate two acres of fertile land, and there is just not enough in Britain to go round. This book shows that from a plot of only twenty square feet, and with just an hour or so's work every week, it is possible to provide supplies of fresh vegetables to feed a small family all the year round, and economise at the same time as leading a healthier life. Happy digging!

Contents

Table of Imperial and Metric Measures

Part 1
Growing Vegetables

Starting Out

1 *Is it true that growing vegetables is hard work?*

You can grow quite useful supplies from a plot only 20 ft square. This need only take an hour or so of work every week.

2 *How much land will I need to feed a family of 2 adults and 2 children?*

To provide all your needs, including potatoes and a fresh vegetable every day of the year, you would need 250-500 sq yds, depending on the fertility of the soil and the skill with which you combine crops.

3 *Surely this would take up a lot of time?*

This depends to a large extent on the soil. Light soils take less work than heavy clays. On average, for such a large production allow at least 10 working hours per week, especially during the growing season.

4 *How could I reduce the work and still obtain good value from a vegetable plot?*

Cut out main-crop potatoes and cabbage, which occupy large areas of land for long periods. Concentrate on small sowings of crops which can be closely planted and which mature rapidly – turnips, peas, beans, lettuce and other salads are examples. You can get some produce all year round, even from a small plot.

5 *What is the ideal site for a vegetable garden?*

A gentle slope towards the south with the shelter of trees, hedges or walls on the north and east sides is best. The slope ensures good drainage and the screen protects against winter winds.

6 *When is the best season for preparing the soil?*

Although you can do this work at any time of year (except in frost and snow), the ideal time is autumn. Once weeds are cleared off, the ground is ready for digging and manuring.

7 *Isn't spring a good time?*

Spring is a little late. It is better to choose open days towards the end of winter, after the winter rains. Soil preparation for vegetable growing must be thoroughly done and if you only have a few hours to spare each week it is likely to take a month or two to get all the plot prepared adequately. If this work is only started in spring the early growth of weeds, which is very vigorous indeed, can be a problem.

8 *Should the season's weed growth be burned?*

Alternatively, make it into compost.

9 *What are the first crops I can put into a vegetable garden prepared in winter?*

You can buy plants of cabbages, lettuce or onions or sow the seeds of peas, beans or spinach. These can be put in from late autumn onwards.

10 *If I cannot finish preparation before spring what then should be the first crops to start?*

Potatoes can be put in, as can quick-maturing crops such as carrots, peas, kidney beans, beetroot, lettuce and so on. For autumn cauliflowers or outdoor tomatoes you have to buy plants. There will also still be time for putting in onions and leeks.

11 *How do I decide where various beds should go?*

Broadly speaking, put seed beds and early crops beside a fence or wall which gets the sun. South- or south-west-facing is ideal. The soil warms up quicker. Divide land in full sun into 3 equal parts (to allow for a rotation of crops). On these you can grow most crops: roots, peas and beans, cabbages and potatoes. Any shaded areas can be used for salads, sea kale and rhubarb. Don't forget a herb bed too, in sun and near the house.

12 *How is it possible to improve the 'climate' within a garden?*

Provide south-facing hedges, fences or walls. Cut back trees that cast heavy shade. Block off cold draughts funnelled through narrow openings between houses. Remove water-logged areas by good drainage and work plenty of dark-coloured material into the soil, such as humus, peat, rotted leaf-mould, and so on. Dark soils retain heat better.

Tools

13 *My new garden has never been cultivated. What tools should I buy first?*

A spade of a weight you find comfortable to handle; a watering can (used to apply weedkillers) and a strong rake. A wheelbarrow is useful, but you can make do with a bucket.

14 *Should I buy a large digging fork?*

This depends on your soil. A fork is easier to use than a spade on heavy land, or for breaking down roughly-dug soil. It is also good for digging out perennial weeds.

15 *Don't I need a hoe?*

You will need one later when growing crops develop. The best type for keeping weeds down is the Dutch or 'push' hoe. A 'draw hoe' (pulled) is good for earthing up, but you can manage without one.

16 *What is a cultivator?*

It is a kind of hoe with several curved prongs. It breaks up compacted soil usefully, especially on medium to light land.

17 *Can flame guns be useful?*

It is possible to use a flame gun over seedbeds (before sowing!). This both destroys small weed seedlings and (to some extent) sterilises the top half inch of soil. It is not by any means a quick or certain operation though. On the whole, these tools tend to be overrated.

18 *What is a dibber?*

Dibbers make holes for planting seedlings etc. Any pointed

9

stick will do. Big kinds are often made from the broken handles of spades and other tools. A useful size is 1¾ in in diameter and about 2 ft long. This is useful for potato planting and making holes for parsnips, etc. Small ones are used for seedlings.

19 *What is dibber watering?*

This is a simple device for watering with a dibber. Make dibber holes about 6-8 in deep, and a few inches away from young plants. Fill these with water, which will gradually soak across to keep their roots supplied.

20 *Should I have my garden dug with a rotovator?*

Provided there are no deep-rooted perennial weeds, a rotovator is fairly satisfactory. Light or medium soils rotovate well. In heavy clays though, especially where the drainage is bad, few rotovators dig deep enough. The machine size is important. Small ones, skilfully used, can dig 8-10 in deep on medium or light soil. On clay, you need a larger machine. No rotovators go as deep as double digging and will not therefore improve drainage much.

21 *Is it worthwhile to buy a rotovator?*

Unless you are going to have a really large vegetable garden a rotovator is not a good buy. You might use it a good deal in the early days, but less and less later on. Of course you can buy rotovators with attachments, such as grass cutters, hedge trimmers and so on. With such a range of tools you will get more working hours from the machine, but it is usually better to hire one.

Soils for Vegetable Growing
22 *What kind of soil do I need to grow vegetables?*

Vegetables will grow on any soil normally found in this country.

23 *But surely some crops need quite different soils from others?*

Only to a small extent and it is only a real problem for big-scale producers where changing the character of a soil on a

10

commercial scale is very expensive. An amateur though can develop a small plot of heavy soil into a lighter type by careful manuring, cultivation and drainage. Too light a soil can be made more water-retaining and fertile by similar processes. For these reasons, amateurs may actually get better results than professional growers.

24 *What different kinds of soil are there?*

For gardening purposes there are light, medium and heavy soils, though there are gradations between the divisions so that one kind blends gradually into another. On the chemical side each of the above types may be either acid or alkaline (limey).

25 *What is the difference between light and heavy soil?*

Not the weight! the term simply refers to the ease or difficulty of cultivating it. Light land is very easy to dig, medium soil rather more difficult, and heavy soil decidedly hard work.

26 *What makes land heavy or light?*

Soil consists of varying proportions of sand, clay, silt, and vegetable matter in various states of decay. There may also of course be buried stones or gravel. The higher the proportion of sand the lighter the soil is. The higher the proportion of clay, the heavier it is. Medium soils have roughly balanced proportions of sand, silt and clay, to make a texture which, whilst draining fairly easily, none the less retains moisture to feed the plants. Most vegetables do best in a medium-weight soil.

27 *How can I change light or heavy land into medium soil?*

Sandy soil can be improved by applying heavy organic stuff such as strawy farmyard manure, or by directly mixing in clay (marl) to add the missing clay ingredient. Heavy clay soils on the other hand can be improved by mixing in rough sands, peat or coarse vegetable matter such as farmyard manure. Digging and liming also break up heavy clays.

28 *Is all medium land fertile?*

By no means. The weight of the soil is only one factor in

fertility. Good soil must also be well-drained, not too acid and contain the proper proportions of organic humus and plant foods.

29 *What is humus?*

Humus is the black, rotted remains of plants that have finally turned to dust. It acts as food for plants and improves the soil texture. It is added to the soil in the form of farmyard manures, peat or compost.

Lime Needs and Application

30 *What does it mean when soil is said to be either acid or alkaline?*

For gardening purposes, it means that lime is short or plentiful. Very acid soils always need lime; alkaline soils never need lime.

31 *Do most new gardens need lime?*

Most soils in this country are acid. The more acid the soil, the more lime you need.

32 *How can I tell how acid my soil really is?*

Buy a soil testing kit. This also shows how much lime is needed to correct the acidity.

33 *Is soil testing a complicated job?*

No; place a pinch of soil into a glass tube and pour the liquid chemicals over it. When the liquid changes colour, match with the chart supplied. This then shows how acid your soil is and how much lime is needed.

34 *Why is it that when I tested my soil I found that some parts of the garden gave different results to other parts?*

Builders scatter lime, cement dust, brick rubble and so on over the soil. Some soil samples may easily contain impurities of this kind. Take several samples of soil that has not been disturbed, from different parts of the garden and also from an inch below the surface. The average result is the figure to use when applying lime.

35 *Is it true that you can tell whether a soil needs lime by looking at the weeds on it?*

Yes; there are some plants, spurrey and sheep's sorrel for example, which only grow on soil which is low in lime. Nowadays though it is better to use a testing outfit.

36 *What exactly does lime do?*

It lowers the acidity of the soil, speeding up the breakdown of natural and artificial fertilisers into liquid chemicals that plants can absorb. On very acid soil, practically no such chemicals are formed and this makes life very hard for plants.

37 *Does this mean it doesn't matter how much lime you put on?*

There is a point at what is known as pH 6.5 where the soil is very slightly acid. At this degree of acidity all the chemical reactions work to the best advantage to plants.

38 *What does pH actually mean?*

Strictly speaking, it means the concentration of electrically charged hydrogen particles. For practical purposes, it measures acidity, where pH 7 is neutral, neither acid nor alkaline. Less than this figure is acid; higher than 7 is alkaline.

39 *Has lime any other benefits?*

It provides calcium which is also good for plants and improves the texture of clay by making the very fine clay particles move together in small pellets. This improves soil ventilation and drainage.

40 *When and how is lime best applied?*

Apply in autumn or very early spring (not later than March 1). Work the lime with a hoe into the top 4 in of soil.

41 *I suppose it is put on at the same time as the other chemical fertilisers that are needed?*

This is not the case; liming and manuring must be at least a month apart, as lime acts on manures to release ammonia, a valuable plant food, which is then lost.

42 Must I apply lime every year?

Not necessarily. No vegetable likes a too alkaline soil. Check acidity regularly and aim for an average of pH 6.5.

43 What plants do best on well-limed soil?

Peas, beans, turnips and cabbage.

44 Do any vegetables tolerate acid conditions?

You can grow potatoes, celery, carrots, rhubarb and seakale on rather more acid soil than most. Lime on potato land may encourage scab disease.

45 Is it correct that lime improves clay soil quite apart from the acidity?

Lime improves the clay texture and helps to rot down buried vegetable matter making potash accessible to plants.

46 If too-acid soils can be improved by adding lime, what makes alkaline soil more acid?

This is technically difficult. Some gardeners apply sulphate of ammonia. This works but the effect disappears after a time. It is better to accept the fact and plan your gardening to avoid plants that dislike lime.

47 Which sort of lime should I use?

Hydrated, powdery lime is easiest to handle. On light soils, ground limestone or ground chalk are better, as they are less easily washed away by rain. You need double the weight compared to hydrated lime.

48 What are quicklime and slaked lime?

They are the same chemical, but in different forms. Quicklime is caustic and must be watered before using it. This changes it to slaked lime, good for heavy clay.

49 How does gypsum improve the soil and what is it?

Gypsum is the chemical calcium sulphate, sometimes used instead of lime. It improves the texture of the soil by removing sodium and replacing it with calcium. Sodium makes soil sticky, but is washed away in drainage water after applying gypsum.

50 *How much is needed?*

Use 6–8 oz per sq yd. It is a good plan to mix this deeply in clay soil, not only into the top few inches.

Cultivation Methods
51 *What cultivation method is best for heavy clay?*

Spade-dig in late autumn, leaving as large lumps as possible and adding lime. Frost will break the clods into smaller particles. During the following season, add plenty of rotted compost, peat or other bulky manures.

52 *What is meant by 'ridging'?*

This method is useful on heavy, wet soils. Throw clods up into long ridges rather than leaving them flat. The aim is to expose the sides of the ridges to the action of the weather, which helps to break down heavy land and improve surface drainage.

53 *I have heard there are soil-conditioning chemicals which will turn clay into good soil, with little work. What are these?*

Some chemicals do break clay up by complex chemical and physical reactions. They are expensive and the results vary depending on the precise state of the original soil.

54 *Why is it that you shouldn't dig heavy soil when it is wet?*

Clays easily pack down to a solid mass, which when dried out becomes almost as hard as rock. A condition like this never grows good plants and may take months to improve again. Treading heavy land in wet weather can ruin its fertility.

55 *In my garden there is an upper layer of dark soil about 6 in deep over a much coarser-looking, pale-coloured soil beneath. Should I mix these together?*

No; plants live almost entirely upon the dark, fine 'topsoil'.

15

Feeding roots spread out into it. Roots do go down into the 'subsoil' beneath, but mainly to seek water and to hold the plant in place. When digging, keep topsoil and subsoil separate.

56 *How can I dig my soil deeply without mixing subsoil and the topsoil?*

By 'double digging'. Dig a trench a foot wide and as deep as the topsoil across one end of your plot. Wheelbarrow this soil to the other end of your plot. Dig over the subsoil at the bottom of the open trench, breaking it up well. Then dig a second trench adjacent to the first but instead of removing the topsoil, throw it forward over the dug subsoil in the first trench. This in turn produces a further trench of exposed subsoil to be dug over. Continue right across the plot. The soil from the first trench is finally used to fill the last trench.

57 *What is bastard trenching?*

This is another name for double digging.

58 *Does all my plot require equally deep digging?*

Deep digging is usually only needed for a few crops, especially 'perennial' kinds (that stay in the same place year after year). The rest of the plot can be dug about a foot deep only, provided the land is reasonably well drained.

59 *What is loam?*

There is no strict definition. It means a medium-weight soil, usually fertile with properly balanced sand, silt, clay and humus. Occasionally, it is also used to mean the soil immediately under old meadow grass which is often of a fibrous texture and full of humus.

60 *I live on a light soil which dries out in summer. How can I improve this?*

Add water-retaining material such as peat, straw, stable manure, leaf-mould, etc., in the top 8 in. It is best to use this liberally on a small section rather than scatter it thinly over the whole plot.

61 *Should I dig this light soil deeply?*

Except to mix in manure there is no advantage in digging up free-draining subsoil.

62 *What is the 'tilth' of a soil?*

Tilth refers to the texture of the soil. Good tilth soil has an open, crumby appearance. Compressed lightly in the hand, it holds together but a light tap breaks it apart into granules. It is usually dark and moist, yet surplus water drains from it easily. Such soil does not become water-logged and delicate roots find it easy to penetrate its moist yet airy conditions.

63 *Does hoeing improve the tilth?*

Besides the obvious value of keeping weeds down by cutting their roots, the slight turning action of the top inch or two of soil improves its aeration, prevents caking in hot sun, improves surface drainage and maintains cooler conditions around the delicate surface roots, especially of young plants.

64 *Why is frost considered good for newly-dug soil?*

Heavy soils contain much water. On freezing, this expands and pushes apart the soil particles. Then as the sun warms the soil the surplus water can drain away, leaving the particles spaced a little apart, thus improving the texture of the soil. It is easier to work with and the roots can penetrate it more quickly.

65 *Can I dig ground when it has snow on it?*

Never dig snow into the soil. Once it is buried it does not melt quickly, lowers the temperature of the soil to a considerable depth and slows the heating action of the spring sun much more than you might expect. Remember that for early seeding you need a warm soil.

66 *Is it all right if I remove most of the snow beforehand?*

It is hard to get rid of all snow, but if you can clear the ground and then allow the remaining sprinkling of snow to be melted naturally you can dig the ground soon afterwards.

2

67 *I have read that some gardeners never dig their ground. How is this possible?*

Wild land is never cultivated yet weeds grow well there! Plants die and leaves fall, to rot gradually down and be worked into the soil by worms, insects and bacteria. The technique of 'no digging' tries to duplicate this natural process and involves year-by-year application of compost to the soil surface. This gradually builds up a very fine, fertile, top layer of soil which plants find very congenial.

Drainage

68 *How can I get rid of the many small stones in my garden soil?*

Why bother? Stones do not normally hinder plant growth except in seed-beds or near young plant-roots. Elsewhere, removal is a matter of appearance, not necessary, and in fact stones can help heavy soil by improving drainage.

69 *Why is garden drainage so important? Surely plants need water to live.*

Plants certainly need water, but their roots must also have air or they cannot grow. They will 'drown' if kept in totally airless, waterlogged conditions. Ideally, soil should contain about the same proportion of free air as it does water, between the soil particles.

70 *Do all gardens need to have actual drainpipes laid out under them?*

Light or stony soils do not usually need any artificial drainage. Medium soil is improved by deep digging. This breaks up hard subsoil to let water through. Heavy soils do require drainage but differ in the amount of water that they retain.

71 *How can I test whether my land is adequately drained or not?*

In spring or autumn (not summer), dig out several holes 2 ft deep in various parts of the garden. They will partially fill with water after rain. If, 24 hours after the rain stops, there is still more than an inch or two of water in the bottom, some drainage is required.

72 Can a soil be too well drained?

Very sandy soils may allow water to pass so rapidly, and leave so much air between the soil particles, that plants cannot get enough water to live on. Heavy dressings of stable manure on sandy soils prevent the rain from draining through too rapidly by acting as a 'sponge'. Applying clay has a similar effect in the long run.

73 What is the simplest form of soil drainage?

Deep digging is the most straightforward, provided it reaches a porous subsoil. By opening up the soil particles it helps the rain to find its way deep into the ground.

74 Would this work on really heavy soil?

Not always; heavy clays are often very deep and you might have to go a long way down before you reached any porous layer. Some other artificial drainage is needed in these conditions.

75 How are pipe drains arranged?

First decide where the water can drain to. Co-operation between neighbouring gardeners is often essential or the water will simply be fed from one plot to another. In the long run, water must be guided either deep underground or into a ditch.

76 As few modern gardeners have ditches nearby, where can the water be guided?

Make a drain soakaway. This is a hole dug down until it reaches a porous layer of soil. Water passing into it soaks down through this layer and away underground.

77 It acts rather like a pond, you mean?

No; it is not a hole to catch and hold water, but a channel through which water escapes downwards. The difference is important. If a hole is dug into a thick clay bed and drain pipes led there, it will certainly fill up so that water still draining in will have nowhere to go. Such a 'drainage' system is useless.

78 *How big should a soakaway be?*

Dig it at least 3 ft square and 4 ft deep, but the depth naturally depends on how deep the porous soil layer lies. In thick clay, soakaways may have to be 7 ft or more deep. Do not dig one this deep yourself however, as the sides may collapse in dangerously.

79 *Should I leave the soakaway as an open hole?*

Fill it to within 18 in of the surface with porous material, broken bricks, clinker, small stones, etc. This allows water to drain through freely. Finally, fill to the top with 6 in of finer gravel and 12 in of fine topsoil.

80 *How are the pipes arranged?*

First dig out trenches leading into your soakaway or ditch. Slope the bottoms of the trenches by at least 1 in 20 from their outer ends to the soakaway. Pipes are normally about 12 in long and 3 in in diameter, laid end to end along the trench bottom, touching but not cemented. Water gets into the drain through the open joints. Cover the pipes with 2 in of fine broken stones or gravel and then refill the trenches to the top with soil.

81 *Is there a cheaper drain system than full-scale piping?*

Dig out trenches sloping towards your soakaway or ditch and then half fill them with broken stones, well rammed down. If you have some turf, lay it upside down on this and then refill with soil. This is fairly effective for small gardens.

Weedkilling
82 *Must I get rid of weeds before I dig my garden?*

This depends on the type of weeds. Annual weeds grown from seeds left over from the previous season can be dug in. First, prevent them seeding by cutting them down before the seeds form. Perennial weeds with deep roots that have been growing for years are best dug out or poisoned and burnt. In both cases, the removed top growth can be rotted down on the compost heap.

20

83 *What are the most effective methods to get rid of perennial weeds?*

Dig them out or poison them. Digging out is heavy work but is the safest method. It is easier to use poison by spraying the ground with a 'total' weedkiller but the disadvantage of this is that the soil cannot be replanted till the poison has washed away.

84 *What are the differences between the many kinds of garden weedkillers?*

In vegetable gardening there are 3 types of weedkiller (perhaps better called plant killers). These are:

surface killers, which are applied to the soil and kill plants as they germinate. These can keep down annual weeds (between perennials for example) or can prevent weeds germinating for a short period before the crop pushes up its first leaves.

contact killers which are applied to the weeds and are absorbed by their leaves. Some of these only act effectively against small annual weeds and so can be used between perennial plants or even between strong-growing annual plants. Some of them can control perennial weeds such as nettles.

total weedkillers which can kill every type of plant (whether crops or weeds). These are only used on paths or drives or on land to be cleared completely of all plants before cultivation starts. This poison often takes several months or even years to vanish completely from the soil.

85 *What are the main types of total weedkillers, used to clear new land for digging?*

Sodium chlorate kills all plants. It is easily purchased at comparatively low cost and is not poisonous. It is however highly inflammable. The other main type is that based on paraquat which kills all weeds but becomes inactive as soon as it reaches the soil. Consequently, cultivation and planting can go on at once. Unfortunately, paraquat is extremely poisonous. It is not available on free sale now except as special commercial preparations of a very weak character. *Always* follow the maker's instructions for weedkillers accurately and above all, *keep them away from children. Never put weedkillers in drink bottles.* To drink raw liquid para-quat (in its strong liquid form) is certain death. *Never* buy weedkillers from farmers or commercial users.

86 *Does sodium chlorate remain active long in the soil?*

For six months afterwards it is not wise to put in any crops.

87 *How valuable are chemical weedkillers in vegetable gardening?*

On large-scale commercial work they have great labour-saving importance. In private gardens though, weeds should not be a significant problem if proper cultivation is being done. Their main use is on paths where total weedkillers can be sprayed saving unprofitable weeding work.

88 *What is a 'pre-emergent' weedkiller?*

This is a weedkiller sprayed over the surface to kill weed seedlings as they break through. The strength of the killer dies away before the main batch of cultivated seedlings germinate.

89 *Is this very difficult to time correctly?*

It isn't really, but it is vital to follow carefully the instructions given by the makers.

90 *Can I simply bury perennial weeds as I dig the ground over, without first using weedkillers?*

This is effective provided that the digging is deep enough. Many weeds such as nettles and docks regrow quickly even when their roots have been buried upside-down and chopped up in pieces! Use double digging, and as each trench is opened, scatter the dug weeds in it, sprinkle a little sulphate of ammonia over them and fork them under.

Compost
91 *What exactly is compost?*

Compost is rotted-down garden and home refuse. Almost anything vegetable or animal (whether cooked or not) can be rotted down. Compost is also the name given to special soil mixtures used for pots and greenhouses.

92 *How valuable is compost outdoors?*

Good compost is one of the most valuable general fertilisers it is possible to get. But it must be properly made. It is no good heaping up rancid rubbish till it is half decomposed and then scattering it about the garden!

93 *What sort of container should compost be made in?*

Ideally, this should be at least 4 ft high and 3 ft square or bigger. It doesn't matter what it is made of provided that it holds the compost securely but allows good ventilation. This is necessary for the bacteria which rot the compost material to work effectively. Try making squares frames of 2 in by 1 in wood, 3 ft square, and cover them with 1 in mesh wire netting. Fasten 4 of these with steel angle brackets to make a bottomless 'box'.

94 *Can compost be made without a container?*

Yes, though the heaps tend to become untidy. Make the pile 3 ft high and 4–5 ft wide at the base.

95 *What sort of things go into compost?*

Almost anything organic – lawn mowings, vegetable remains, leaves, food waste and so on.

96 *Is the rubbish just tipped in and left undisturbed?*

No; start by placing very coarse material (even small logs) in the bottom to give good aeration. Add a 4 in layer of somewhat finer material to prevent the compost itself from dropping through. Add a 6 in layer of compost material, spread out level. Sprinkle a handful of sulphate of ammonia on to this and stir it in gently with a fork to speed up rotting.

97 *Do I need any special method of starting the rotting process?*

Rotting will often start without any assistance but you can tip half a bucket of any type of farmyard or horse manure on the bottom layer. Bacteria from this will start the rot from the base up. Moisture is vital, so keep compost wetted both on stacking and while it rots down.

98 *What about proprietary rotting compounds?*

These give good results. They provide food for the bacteria that rot down the compost, just like the sulphate of ammonia we mentioned above.

99 *Is it desirable to mix soil with compost?*

Yes; between each 6 in layer of rubbish, spread 2 in of ordinary fine soil over the heap. This 'sandwich' effect greatly improves the compost. On most soils except chalk, sprinkle lime in this soil layer, or the compost may be rather acid.

100 *Can the pile then be left to itself?*

You must 'turn' the heap after 4–6 weeks. Dig the compost from the container and replace it after mixing it thoroughly. This helps to rot the outer parts of the heap as well as the interior.

101 *How long should I leave it?*

Leave for roughly a further 6–8 weeks, but remember that the process is slower in cold periods. You can reckon on getting good compost within about 4 months of starting.

102 *Does it need special protection in store?*

It is always best to use compost fairly soon after its rotting process is complete. For various reasons its nitrogen content may then be higher. If you do store it, protect it from the rain since nitrogen tends to be washed out by water.

103 *My new garden is on meadow. Should I dig the turf in?*

Turf is always buried as it rots quickly to good compost.

104 *I have used a selective weedkiller on my lawn. This has been very effective, but I wonder if it is safe to use the clippings for composting?*

These might be safe by the time they have rotted down but, on the whole, it is better to burn them, using the ashes as a fertiliser instead.

105 *I suppose leaf-mould is a kind of compost, and made in a similar way?*

Most kinds of leaves make good compost. Oak and beech especially can be stored in a separate heap to give a fine mould. Chestnut leaves take longer to rot down than the other smaller types.

106 Does leaf mould differ from other composts?

If made entirely from leaves it resembles peat, improves water-retaining capacity in the soil and adds humus. Use it particularly if the soil is alkaline.

107 How long does it take for fresh leaves to rot down to a good mould?

A whole year. Leave them heaped up in a wire-netting enclosure.

108 Can't I simply dig the leaves into the ground instead of rotting them down in this way?

This is possible but not quite so effective. It still takes a long time for the leaves to rot down in the soil. Either method though is better than wasting leaves by burning them.

109 The 'no digging' plan, using all compost, must take a great deal of material?

Yes; there is also a lot of work in preparing, mixing and distributing it. In the long run though, it produces a wonderful soil.

Manures and Fertilisers

110 Do the words manure and fertiliser mean the same thing?

Usually the word manure is used for natural or 'organic' products, whilst fertiliser is used for raw chemicals. Some products such as bonemeal are made by grinding up natural organics and for these either word can be used.

111 What does 'organic' mean?

For gardeners organic manures are those made from natural, living products, as against the *inorganic*, which are raw chemicals, mined or manufactured.

112 *Which are best for plants, chemical fertilisers or organic manures?*

Plants live only on chemicals which they extract from the soil. How the chemicals get there does not matter. 'Artificial' chemicals are immediately usable by plants as food. Organics must be altered in the soil, by bacteria, acidity and so on, to release their chemicals. However, plants also need a soil that is soft and friable, and includes adequate air and moisture, and improvement of these is easiest done by giving bulky natural manures. A combination of both gives the best results.

113 *What are the main plant foods?*

Most important are nitrogen, phosphorus, potassium and magnesium. They are usually given as nitrates, phosphates and potash which are represented by the letters N, P and K respectively on bags of chemical fertilisers.

114 *What is the main function of nitrogen?*

It helps leafy growth and the green colour of leaves. Consequently, though all plants need nitrogen to some extent, it is chiefly used for lettuce, cabbage, cauliflower, etc., where leaf growth is the main aim. Lack of nitrogen stunts plants and lightens or blues the leaves.

115 *What purpose do the other 3 chemicals serve?*

Phosphorus strengthens roots and helps flowers and fruit to ripen. It helps the production of sugar and starch in the plant and has other functions connected with its general health. Stunted roots are a sign of phosphate shortage. Magnesium forms part of the green colouring of the leaves. Lack of it causes leaves to turn yellow or discolour. Potassium encourages stems, improves plant health and better fruits.

116 *What are the main nitrogen fertilisers?*

These may be quick or slow acting. In general, quick-acting ones are used in spring and summer to give a boost to growth, or later in the year when a final swift stimulant is needed. Slower kinds are applied in autumn or winter and become available to the plants throughout the early spring and summer. The quickest-acting sorts are ammonium sulphate

(21% N), especially useful on neutral or alkaline soils; nitrate of soda (16% N), nitro chalk, useful on very acid soils; calcium cyanamide (21% N), good for acid soils or compost making; urea (36% N), suitable for normal or alkaline soil but mainly used for liquid fertilisers; dried blood (13% N), useful for any soil. The best slower-acting kind is hoof and horn meal (14% N), which acts steadily over a fairly long period, and is useful in any soil.

117 Is soot water any good as a fertiliser?

This can be useful as a minor nitrogen stimulant. All garden soot has to be heaped outdoors to 'weather' for several months before use. Wrap a pound or two in a cloth bag and drop for a few days into a 2 gal tub of water. The liquid (not the sediment) is added to your watering water giving it a light brown colour.

118 What value has dry soot?

It contains a little nitrogen, but needs to be heavily supplied at about 6–8 oz per sq yd. Its main use is to darken the colour of soil so that it absorbs heat more easily in spring. It also keeps slugs away.

119 What about phosphorus fertilisers?

These are graded according to how much phosphoric acid (soluble in water) they contain. Again, they may be slow or fast acting. Quick sorts are superphosphate (18% P) for any soil and good for starting off plants; and mono-ammonium phosphate (62% P), better for neutral or alkaline soils and mainly used for liquid manures. Slower sorts are basic slag (variable from 8% P to 18% P), very slow acting but cheap and good for winter digging and new ground, especially on clays or acid soil; bonemeal and hoof and horn meal for use in winter; steamed boneflour (27% P), moderately slow, for use in late winter and spring and very good for seed beds.

120 What is basic slag?

It is produced in steel works when the slag from phosphorus in iron ores combines with the lime and magnesia used in the furnaces. It is then treated and ground up for use as a fertiliser.

121 *Can basic slag be used on light soil?*

Certainly, and especially if you give a potash fertiliser as well to widen its effect.

122 *Are there different grades?*

There is a wide variation in the amount of actual usable phosphoric acid. (This is given on the bag.) First-class basic slag is 80% citric acid soluble and is very finely ground indeed.

123 *How much should be given?*

Anything up to ½ lb per sq yd.

124 *What are the advantages of the bone phosphates?*

Bonemeal and hoof and horn meal are useful because, being very slow acting, they release phosphates gently into the soil so that it is practically impossible to over-treat.

125 *How much bonemeal is usually needed?*

Use about 4–6 oz per sq yd. Hoof and horn meal is usually limited to 2 oz per sq yd.

126 *What is the main chemical source of potash?*

Potash fertilisers are graded according to their content of potassium oxide. Quick-acting ones are sulphate of potash (48% K), useful at any time on most soils except very acid ones; muriate of potash (50% K, but including up to 15% salt), which must be kept off clay because the salt spoils the texture of the land; nitrate of potash (45% K and 12–14% N) is mainly used for liquid manure. Slower-acting kinds are Chilean potash nitrate (14% K but including also 10–15% nitrogen), good for all but very acid soils, and especially useful on sandy, light ones; Kainit (14% K) is applied in autumn and also contains magnesium. Wood ashes (not household fuel ashes) also give potash, but the amount is variable between 2% and 7%. Ashes can be used at any time on most soils, but contain calcium and may make the soil more alkaline.

127 *How do I know what proportion of each fertiliser to give?*

Fertilisers are often sold as 'general' fertilisers already containing balanced proportions of nitrogen, phosphorus, potash and magnesium. Others have rather more of one or other of the constituents and these specialised fertilisers are for use on particular crops.

128 *Can you recommend a simple mixture for a home-made general fertiliser?*

Use 4 lb hoof and horn meal, 2 lb bonemeal, 2 lb superphosphate and 2 lb sulphate of potash. Mix these together and use at about 4 oz per sq yd. This gives a good start to most vegetables, especially if you supplement it later with liquid manures.

129 *Do any plants benefit by being given more of any particular chemical?*

Fertile soil will grow most plants reasonably well but to reach perfection some may need additional foods. Plants needing potash and nitrogen are particularly the roots group – carrots, parsnips, radish and beets. Crops needing phosphates and nitrogen are those grown for leaves – cabbage, sprouts, broccoli, lettuce, etc. Crops needing phosphates and potash are the pea and bean group and potatoes. Incidentally, the legumes (peas and beans) need *less* nitrogen because unlike most plants they can get this from the air.

130 *Are fertilisers best applied dry or as liquids?*

All plants take up their food in liquid form, so in theory liquids should be slightly better. However, liquids can also drain rapidly away, especially in light land. Provided the weather is showery and the soil moist, dry chemicals will soon be dissolved.

131 *What are pelleted fertilisers?*

These are chemicals which have been formed into pellets. They can be distributed more accurately and evenly, often by mechanical means. You can even put individual pellets by individual plants.

132 *Why is farmyard manure so well thought of by gardeners?*

Farm or stable manure contains the main chemical fertilisers and lots of humus. It greatly improves the texture of the soil, especially if made with straw. Most soil can absorb almost unlimited quantities of farmyard manure and be all the better for it. So it is almost impossible to over-apply. This is not true of the chemical fertilisers which must be strictly controlled in quantity.

133 *When is farmyard manure applied?*

In spring on medium or light soils but on heavy soils during autumn or winter digging.

134 *I have bought some farm manure but I have been told I must not use it fresh.*

This is correct. Store it under a temporary cover (but let air get in to the heap). Cover it with 6 in of soil if possible and spread after 8 weeks.

135 *I would have thought root crops would benefit from plenty of farm manure, so why have I been told not to apply it before planting?*

Unless the manure is very deeply buried it tends to cause root crops to divide instead of forming a single root. The growing tip of a carrot may fork into two or three points seeking the nearby rich manure.

136 *Treated sewage sludge is offered for sale by our local council. This does not sound very pleasant. Is it good stuff?*

This is one of the most valuable of fertilisers for its price, especially on light soils. It contains humus and all 3 of the main fertilisers and it does not smell!

137 *What are fish and hop manures and how valuable are they?*

Fish manure is simply dried fish wastes with the addition of chemicals. It has to be used according to the directions. Hop manure too is a manufactured fertiliser, using dried hops as a base.

138 *Is hop manure the same as 'spent hops'?*

No; spent hops are used hops delivered straight from the brewery. They do not contain much plant food, but they are a good source of humus. They can be used instead of peat, a bucketful per sq yd.

139 *Has seaweed any value as a fertiliser?*

Certain makers market seaweed fertilisers which can be used according to the directions. Seaweed itself contains all 3 fertilisers though in very small quantities. You need a large amount to make any effect, say 10–20 lb per sq yd (weighed wet).

140 *Is sawdust a good fertiliser?*

Never put sawdust directly into the soil before it has rotted down. The bacteria which cause it to rot actually live on the nitrogen in the soil itself and so reduce the amount available for the crops. Instead, mix sawdust into the compost heap and feed the bacteria with sulphate of ammonia – a handful to every 3–4 in depth.

141 *What is the best use for sawdust compost?*

Scatter as a top dressing over the soil surface fairly thickly in April and June. Give a little nitrogen at the same time, such as a dusting of nitro chalk.

142 *How valuable is poultry manure?*

This is a rich organic manure, rather too strong for direct use in the soil and best mixed 50-50 with compost or fine soil. Store it a week or two before using.

143 *What plant food value has peat?*

Practically none; but peat benefits both light and heavy soils by improving the texture. In heavy soils the particles of peat prevent the clay from compacting into an impenetrable mass. Peat bonds light soils together, provides a moisture reserve and so prevents rainwater from carrying away valuable food chemicals too quickly.

144 *What is the best natural manure for sandy soil?*

To improve its texture and water-retaining capacity cow manure is almost ideal. You need a lot though to make a significant impression.

145 *What is guano?*

In certain parts of the world seabirds have lived for centuries and their droppings have accumulated to enormous depths. These are a very valuable fertiliser, rather similar to poultry manure. It is bought through the trade, usually with instructions on the amounts required. The quality varies somewhat from place to place.

146 *What is shoddy?*

Shoddy is waste produced by wool factories and is good for most gardens if dug in during early winter. It provides nitrogen and humus.

147 *Besides the main fertilisers of nitrogen, phosphorus and potassium, what others are required in quantity?*

Calcium (usually provided by lime), magnesium and iron are needed.

148 *A friend recommends giving Epsom salts to plants sometimes. Surely this cannot be right?*

Sulphate of magnesium is quite correctly used to adjust a magnesium deficiency, at about $\frac{1}{2}$ oz per gall of water.

149 *Is it true that some soils don't contain iron and plants suffer from this?*

Nearly all soils do contain iron but not always in a form which is easily accessible to plants. This is sometimes the case in alkaline soils such as chalk.

150 *Do any vegetables suffer from iron deficiency in these cases?*

Few vegetables like alkaline soils, but iron deficiency is not normally a problem in amateur vegetable gardening.

151 *Is it possible to compensate for iron deficiency?*

There are special chemicals which may be used around very valuable plants such as rhododendron shrubs but it is not worthwhile to bother with them for vegetables.

152 *What are trace elements?*

These are chemicals needed by plants in very small amounts – manganese, boron, zinc, copper and molybdenum. Most soils in this country already contain enough of each.

153 *Is sulphur required?*

Not as a rule and in any case it forms part of many common fertilisers.

154 *Do any vegetables require salt as a fertiliser?*

It is a long standing tradition to scatter 1 oz per sq yd in spring over asparagus beds, and to give it to seakale.

155 *Are liquid manures simply dry chemicals dissolved in water?*

Yes; except urine, which some farmers collect from their cowhouse drains. Different chemicals are used of course for different purposes.

156 *How is liquid manure given?*

Do not pour liquid manure directly over any plant. Strong chemical can affect the leaves. A good tip is to make shallow holes with a dibber right alongside the plants, but 6 in away. Pour liquid manure into these holes, and it will seep gradually out to feed the roots nearby.

157 *After watering my plants with a chemical manure I found marks on the leaves as if the spots had burnt them. Could this be the manure?*

Any moist chemical (even fertiliser) can damage leaves. If you cannot keep the manure from the leaves, try spraying afterwards with clear water. This washes off or weakens any traces of fertiliser.

158 *What is green manuring?*

This is a process in which crops of very rapidly developing

3

plants are grown and then dug into the ground. As the plants rot they provide valuable fertiliser. Sowing is often done in August for digging in during October or November.

159 *When green manuring, do different soils require different plants?*

Any plants are helpful, but in general, on light soil use lupins, on heavy soil, farmer's vetch and on very alkaline (chalk) soils, mustard and clover help.

160 *How exactly are the manure plants treated?*

Allow all the plants to grow until the flower buds show. With all but lupins this is usually at 6–12 in high. Then trample all over the plants, scatter the sulphate of ammonia (on alkaline soils) or nitro chalk and after a week dig the whole lot into the ground.

161 *How can I use lupins to make a good green manure?*

Lupins are legumes so the roots contain nitrogen and soil benefits from this as well as from the rotting down of the green leaves. Ordinary cheap sorts can be sown in spring and rapidly develop into substantial plants. Sow seed at about ½ oz per sq yd and turn the lupin seedlings into the ground in autumn as soon as they begin to flower.

162 *Does it improve the results to give fertiliser too?*

Scatter sulphate of ammonia or nitro chalk at up to 2 oz per sq yd into the topsoil whilst turning over the ground.

Rotation of Crops
163 *I have heard that vegetables must be grown in some system of 'rotation'. What exactly does this mean?*

Rotation simply means planting different crops in 3 successive seasons and then returning to the first crop. The soil has a 2-year 'rest' from each particular crop.

164 *What then are the main reasons for following rotation plans?*

Closely related crops such as peas and beans or the various types of cabbage often suffer from the same general types of
34

diseases. An infected plant can contaminate the soil and pass on the disease to any similar plant which follows it. By rotating crops, the contaminated soil becomes cleared by cultivation and the growth of other crops. Different plants have different food needs, and remove different chemicals from the soil. Changing them each year evens up the use of the soil chemicals. Legumes help the following leafy crops by providing nitrogen.

165 Do all vegetables need rotation of this kind?

No; you can grow potatoes, onions and cabbage for two or three seasons on the same plot. Scarlet runner beans, rhubarb, artichokes and asparagus can grow in the same position, year after year, without harm.

166 How do I plan the rotation of my crops?

Roughly speaking, there are three groups of vegetables.
Leaf crops: broccoli, brussels sprouts, cabbage, cauliflower, kale, savoys, spinach (but not lettuce).
Roots: beetroot, carrots, celeriac, kohl-rabi, parsnips, potatoes, salsify, scorzonera, swedes, turnips.
Seeds, Stems and Bulbs: beans, peas, celery, endive, leeks, onions, radishes, shallots.
Divide your land into 3 equal sections, 1 for each group. The second season all the groups move: the leaf crops that were on plot 1 move to take the place of the roots on plot 2. Roots move to plot 3 and seeds, etc., move to plot 1. The third year all move once again, and by the fourth year all are back to their original plots.

167 Does this mean I can only grow one crop per year on the land?

The rule given is only a general one. You can increase the yields from each plot by intensive culture, growing more than one crop on the same plot during a single season.

168 What crops will permit this growing of a second crop?

Any early-maturing vegetables such as early turnips, onions, cabbage, potatoes and of course the early peas. These are all cleared in time to get a subsequent crop in.

169 *What crops should I choose to follow these early-maturing crops?*

You need vegetables which will come to maturity within a comparatively short time; for instance lettuce, spinach, onions, carrots and perhaps turnips, cabbages or broccoli (which would remain in position till the succeeding spring).

170 *How is manuring related to the rotation plan?*

Leaf crops: Give lime (usually) and general fertiliser just before sowing seeds (but on plots previously growing legumes less nitrogen will be needed).
Root crops: Apply mixed fertilisers.
Seeds, Stems and Bulbs: Apply organic manures such as farm manures or compost.

171 *What is a 'catch crop'?*

This is a very rapidly-maturing crop which can be planted between rows of vegetables which grow more slowly. Sometimes you can put such a second crop between the plants of another crop in the same row.

172 *Can you give one or two examples?*

Between rows of beans you can plant brussels sprouts; between cabbages, the coleworts; between cauliflowers, lettuce or spinach; between rows of celery you can grow lettuce, dwarf early peas, endives or french beans. Between rows of kidney beans and peas you can grow many kinds such as spinach, radishes, broccoli, lettuce, turnips, very early carrots or brussels sprouts. Between potato rows it is more difficult because they have to be earthed up. However, after this has been done you can interplant with some of the cabbage family.

173 *Are there plants which you cannot interplant in this way with catch crops?*

In general do not put other crops between rows of the catch crops themselves as listed above. Not, for example, between rows of beet, broccoli, carrots, parsnips, lettuce, onions, leeks, turnips or spinach.

174 *What is intensive culture?*

Any garden organisation that makes the best possible use of every inch of cultivated ground, throughout as long a season as possible, as in the catch crop system for instance. Intensive also often refers to starting crops as seedlings between rows of crops that are approaching maturity. It is even possible to have 3 entirely different crops occupying the same piece of land at once, each of the crops being at different degrees of maturity.

175 *How can I plan the intensive culture of a small vegetable garden?*

This requires skill in timing and in selection of crops. It is also vital to adjust plantings to suit the weather conditions at the time and not to work slavishly by the plan (or calendar). Much will also depend on what you aim to produce. There would not be much value in intensive culture which delivered to the kitchen large quantities of vegetables which were not really required, or at the wrong time of year.

176 *Can you give some examples of multiple cropping?*

Interplant potatoes and greens such as brussels sprouts. A more advanced plan would be to sow runner beans between alternate potato rows in early summer, keeping the beans pinched down to 2 ft high. Then as the potatoes are lifted towards the end of summer put late cauliflowers in their place immediately, between the now developing rows of runner beans. When these 2 crops are themselves cleared in autumn the ground can be occupied by winter lettuce.

177 *I have heard of growing tomatoes between potatoes. Is this a good plan?*

In fact you can even graft a tomato on top of a potato to make the 'tomtato', with potatoes on the roots and tomatoes on the shoots. The trouble is that neither do as well as the two crops independently. You can put tomatoes between potatoes (after these have been finally earthed up) but you need first-class cultivation for this. Any trace of disease on the potatoes will be passed on immediately to the tomatoes, which are close relatives. After both crops have been cleared, lettuce can be planted or perhaps spring cabbage.

178 *What are legumes?*

Legumes are pod-seeding plants like peas, beans or lupins.

179 *How are they useful in the rotation plan?*

Legumes have the rare capacity to obtain nitrogen from the air around us. Nitrogen is a valuable fertiliser and is then stored in small lumps or 'nodules' on the roots of the plant. When the crop has been harvested, the tops can be cut away but the roots should be left in the ground to rot away. This releases the nitrogen as a fertiliser for the following crop. If this is a cabbage crop (as it should be) which requires plentiful nitrogen to make leaves, you can easily see the advantage.

Seeds

180 *Why are there so many varieties of vegetables? Is there really much difference between them?*

Yes; varieties differ in whether they like light, medium or heavy soil; whether they are early, moderate or late maturing; whether they are hardy or only partially hardy; whether they give large individual heads or a bulk of smaller heads (where this is applicable). Some varieties crop heavily on poor land; others crop best on rich land; others may have different flavours. When you know your soil type, decide what type of crop you want and ask the advice of a reputable seedsman.

181 *How can I tell how much seed to buy?*

Seeds vary tremendously in size, so obviously an ounce of seed of different plants will not always fill the same length of row. When you buy large seeds such as peas they are often sold by the 'pint' but most others in $\frac{1}{4}$ oz steps or small packets. With each main vegetable we have given the amount of seed you will need.

182 *Can you give me some brief examples?*

If you can buy an ounce of the following seeds you can sow approximately the length of drill shown: turnips, 40 yd; radishes, 25 yd; parsley, 40 yd; parsnips, 50 yd; lettuce, 60 to 70 yd; onions, 50 yd; carrots, 30 yd; beetroot, 20 yd.

183 *What about cabbage?*

You can get at least 5,000 plants from every ounce of cabbage seed and rather more from leeks, whilst the tiny celery seed gives anything up to 50,000 plants to the ounce. Obviously, you would not buy such large quantities!

184 *I have seen a number of gardening calendars giving dates for sowing seeds, reaping, harvesting and so on, but they don't always agree. Is there a reliable calendar of this kind?*

It is impossible to give dates on which garden jobs should be done. Dates of sowing depend on the ground being warm enough, containing the right amount of moisture, on the duration and strength of sunshine, on the type of fertility of soil and the plant variety. Clearly these vary from north to south of the country and even with individual gardens.

185 *How can temperature and moisture vary within one garden?*

A wall or fence positioned to the north of a bed not only provides shelter from cold winds, but also deflects the sun's rays down on to the soil. In such a south-facing bed seeds may germinate 2–3 weeks early. As for moisture, some parts of a garden are bound to be better-drained than others.

186 *I suppose drainage also depends on the type of soil?*

Yes; light, sandy soils warm up quicker because the water evaporates easily through the large pores of the soil. In heavy clay water has difficulty in evaporating or draining away, and so it may take weeks more to dry out ready for seeding.

187 *Do differing weather conditions year by year make much difference?*

The average conditions in any part of the country are similar year to year, and especially in parts near the sea. However, this average does not mean that every year is the same. There may be a variation of up to 2–3 weeks in different years in the dates when a plot is ready for seeding.

188 *How important is the height of the garden above sea level?*

High gardens are colder, though often brighter. This increased sunshine may compensate.

189 *Is there any other aspect of soil type which affects seeding time?*

Colour plays a significant part. Dark soils absorb heat more readily and warm up more quickly in the sun. Many gardeners scatter dark peat or soot over the land in order to retain sun heat.

190 *How can I tell when the soil is warm enough to sow seeds?*

Use a soil thermometer which is not an expensive item. Make checks 2–3 in below the surface. Most seeds like peas and beans need about 10°C (50°F) as a minimum.

191 *For general later sowing, what soil temperature is needed?*

As the temperature rises above 15° C (59°F), usually in March, you can begin sowing in earnest. If in doubt, watch the outdoor shrubs and hedges. When their buds start to burst, growth has started.

192 *Is there any quick rule of thumb about the depth for sowing seed?*

It depends largely on the size of the seed. Very small seeds are only just sprinkled over with soil or fine sand. Bigger seeds like parsnips can go an inch deep, peas rather deeper and broad and runner beans as deep as 3–4 in.

193 *In which direction should rows of seeds and plants be set?*

Plant north to south, so that each plant receives an equal amount of sun on both sides and they do not shade each other so much.

194 *How can I help my seeds to germinate?*

Many seeds die through fungus attack before they appear above ground, so apply a preventive preseeding treatment such as a thyram. This is often a powder dropped in the seed packet and shaken.

195 *What sort of seeds should be treated in this way?*

Almost all vegetables can be treated, but the pea and bean family, the brassicas, onions and spinach especially need treatment.

196 *Should I tread down the soil after seeding?*

The seed-bed must be firm and close enough to allow roots to develop without pushing the seeds up above the surface. Young roots cannot cross big air spaces in the soil. However, on heavy land treading can cause soil to consolidate to an impenetrable mass. Broadly speaking, tread firmly on light land but very little on heavy, and certainly not when wet.

197 *Why do some old gardeners lay planks over newly seeded drills?*

This helps seeds which may be slow to germinate by providing the darkness seeds prefer and conserving moisture. However, the planks must be taken away as soon as the leaves start to appear, so inspect daily.

198 *How long will seeds be before they appear?*

This varies with the type, the season, the warmth of the soil and sowing conditions generally. On average you can take the following periods: parsley, 30 days; beetroot, 20 days; onions, 20 days; parsnips, 20 days; leeks and carrots, about a fortnight; cabbages, cauliflowers, savoys and turnips, a week or sometimes less; radishes, 2–3 days.

199 *How can I keep track of where I sow my seeds, especially when they don't come up quickly?*

Mark the row ends with pegs so that you have the line to guide you, or try mixing a few cheap seeds of a quick-germinating type such as radish or cress with the main seeds as you sow them. These will come up to mark the rows until the main seedlings appear.

Seedlings

200 *When should seedlings be thinned?*

Many plants send up first two smooth, rounded leaves which
are in fact food supplies and part of the original seed. Above
them will appear the true leaves, often rougher in texture.
Thin the seedlings as soon as the first true leaves appear.

201 *I find it difficult to get even spacing between my plants and at the same time save the best growers. Should I move the plants in order to get them evenly spaced?*

Spacings for plants are not hard and fast. Much depends on
the fertility of the soil. Certainly, never sacrifice a sturdy
plant for a weak one just because the weak one happens to be
in the right place. It is better to move the sturdy plant carefully, taking plenty of soil with it, to the desired spot.

202 *Where is the best place to store seed?*

Avoid damp conditions. Totally dry containers may themselves cause seed to lose its natural moisture, so don't let them
get too hot. A dry, cool box or jar is ideal, kept somewhere
which does not suffer from extremes of temperature.

203 *How can I store seed in packets that have already been opened?*

Seal the packet tops and put them, entire, into tins.

204 *Can I save my own seed for vegetables?*

Generally speaking this is not a good idea. Seed is not very
expensive in relation to the crops you get and it is very hard
for amateurs to recognise when seeds are fully ripe or to be
sure of getting sound types.

205 *How long can seeds be stored before losing the power to germinate?*

This varies tremendously from plant to plant. Beet for
example will still germinate after 10 or more years. As a
general rule though the percentage of seeds germinating
drops with time, so always buy fresh seed whenever possible.

206 *Are the plants themselves less vigorous when grown from old seed?*

Provided the seeds have been stored properly and especially if they have been kept at low temperatures, there is no difference in the plants that germinate. Some sorts even do better from old seed.

207 *When should thinning be done?*

The time to thin is after the first *true* leaves appear. Many plants produce two rounded leaves first, followed by the true leaves.

208 *I often lose young seedlings on transplanting – are there any tips about this?*

Thoroughly water the plants to be moved the day before. Make sure the ground for them is also soaked a few hours before transplanting. Scatter an inch of good, moist compost on the soil to help the water remain near the roots of the plants. Make certain that some soil clings to the roots as you lift the seedlings and don't delay putting them in. If they flag on the surface with their roots exposed they are likely to die.

209 *How deep are seedlings put in?*

Broadly speaking, as deep as they were in the nursery bed, or a little more.

210 *How big a hole should I make?*

Obviously this depends on the size of the plant, but make one big enough to accept the roots spread out.

211 *How should I get the roots into position?*

The best method is to use your fingers so as to avoid damaging the roots. If you do use a tool, take care not to cut through the roots as you press soil round them.

212 *What is a 'hung' plant?*

A seedling whose roots are suspended in the air near the bottom of a planting hole. It is vital that all the fine feeding roots should touch the soil. Work soil round them with the fingers.

213 *Should I sow or transplant vegetables into long rows across my whole plot, or into small patches?*

There is much to be said for growing vegetables in small patches. This sounds odd but there is evidence that plants grow better in company. It may also make fertilisation by insects a little easier.

214 *What is the main disadvantage of patch-growing instead of rows?*

An attack by insect pests or disease on one part of a row may be more easily isolated than in a compact patch.

215 *Why is black polythene sometimes spread flat over the surface of the ground round plants?*

Weeds cannot germinate in the darkness underneath the polythene so it acts like a weedkiller. However, the damp atmosphere underneath sometimes encourages mildews. The plants are put in through holes slashed cross-wise in the plastic.

216 *What is 'hardening off' of seedlings?*

This involves accustoming plants to cold outdoor conditions when they have been seeded under glass. It is done by introducing more air and lowering the temperature of the glasshouse until the plant can do without protection altogether.

Protection from Cold

217 *I realise that planting out and seed sowing should not be done in frost, but how can I tell when frost is likely to occur?*

A cloudless evening after a sunny day can be menacing. Air warmed during the day rises in the evening and currents of heavier, cold air are drawn in underneath near the ground. If your garden is in a hollow, it will naturally accumulate the heaviest, coldest air.

218 *As the seedlings grow, which sorts will need continuing protection against frost?*

Early frosts may curtail the growth season of runner and french beans.

219 *As winter approaches, presumably some kinds will need protection again?*

Yes, but some need no protection. Savoy, cabbage, celery, salsify and carrots are all improved by frost.

220 *How can I protect outdoor plants from cold?*

To keep off cold winds from tall plants hang polythene sheets on the windward side of the rows. Use moveable hurdles of trellis or wattle or hang sacks over ropes stretched between posts. For low-growing crops, glass or plastic cloches are first-class.

221 *What are cloches?*

These are sheets of glass fitted together, usually with wire clips. They may be simple, 2-sheet types, held at the ridge, like an inverted 'V'. More elaborate kinds have vertical side sheets too, like miniature barns. Some of these can be tall enough even for tomatoes.

222 *As they are open at the ends, surely cloches cannot protect plants much from wind?*

Always block off the ends with a sheet of glass or even cardboard. (Small gaps between the cloches themselves are much less trouble and indeed may help with the ventilation.)

223 *How can I improve frost protection under cloches in really cold spells?*

Cover them with several layers of newspaper held down by weighted strings. Put these on in the evening and remove them next day. You can also earth up the sides of the cloches to some extent.

224 *Besides frost protection, what do I gain by using cloches?*

Roughly speaking, every outdoor seeding, transplanting or harvesting job be done a month earlier under cloches. If outdoor sowings are done, say, in May you could sow in April under cloches.

225 *Are the cloches kept shut all the time?*

No; ventilation is as important to plants as protection from frost. Growing under cloches requires similar care with ventilation and watering as does growth in more complicated frames or greenhouses. Dark, humid conditions are often more damaging to seedlings than even a slight dry frost.

226 *How can I control ventilation under rows of cloches?*

Move them or twist them slightly to make gaps at their ends. You can also remove a few panes at intervals along the row. Tomato cloches are specially made with removable sides.

227 *If any of my plants do get frosted can I help them in any way?*

You can try spraying them at once with clear, *cold* water as early as possible in the morning. This helps them to thaw out without bursting the cells (which usually does the damage) when the sun gets up.

228 *When are the cloches put out?*

If used for seeding, place them in position about 2 weeks before the seed is sown. This raises the temperature of the soil beneath.

229 *How do I set out cloches on sloping ground?*

If possible, across the slope, not up and down.

230 *What is a hot-bed?*

Giving even earlier results than cloches, a hot-bed is a special seed-bed prepared with a base of partly-rotted manure. During further rotting, the manure generates heat which warms the fine soil above. This speeds up rooting and generally quickens the development of seeds or cuttings.

231 *How is a hot-bed made?*

It is quite a large job. Dig out a hole at least 2 yd square and about 3 ft deep. Fill the hole with fresh stable manure that has been stored for only a week or two. This will gradually settle a few inches, so fill it up to ground level again with leaves or grass cuttings and a shallow layer of fine earth. Bring this earth 6 in above ground level. If possible surround the raised bed with timber and lay a glass garden frame across the top. If glass is not available use polythene sheeting stretched double over a light-weight frame.

232 *It is hard to imagine there would be much heat from just rotting manure!*

A great deal of heat is in fact generated, more than enough to start off even very tender seeds.

233 *When is the job best done?*

Hot-beds only remain warm for about 6 weeks, so prepare them from February to late March, according to your district. Aim for the heat to be dying away as the danger of frost recedes.

234 *After this, can the hot-bed be used for other plants?*

Yes, lush growers such as marrows welcome planting on such a bed. Keep them well watered.

Watering
235 *How many vegetable crops will require watering?*

Root crops and most of the cabbages hardly ever need watering. Those that need most are rapid-growing plants with fine roots near the surface. In dry weather, peas, beans and celery all need water to continue vigorous growth.

236 *What about young seedlings?*
If there is a long dry spell soon after the seedlings have germinated, then watering will certainly be required, probably every day.

237 *Are there ways of reducing the need to water plants every day?*

Keep the Dutch hoe moving in the top inch or two of soil, so maintaining an open texture and preventing caking. Water loss from the surface will then be reduced. Spread a mulch of peat or compost over the hoed surface at least an inch or two thick. Soak this and it will provide a kind of 'sponge' keeping a moist atmosphere around the plants for 2 or more days.

238 *How should I give water to plants; little and often or a big soaking at less frequent intervals?*

A soaking is always best. Occasional light waterings tend to cause surface rooting and these roots rapidly dry out if the weather becomes hot, doing the plant more harm than good. Never give less than a bucket to every square yard for best results.

239 *Surely it is impossible to water an entire garden at this rate in a day?*

Probably not, but if it is done systematically so that each part gets a thorough soaking once a week this will be the equivalent of having a half-inch rainfall. This is usually enough to keep the plants growing, especially if you also use a surface mulch.

240 *Is rain water better than tap water?*

There is no evidence for this. It might sometimes be warmer. Some commercial water supplies have added chemicals but these are not of a kind likely to affect plants.

241 *Is any particular time of day best for watering?*

It is safe to water any time but evaporation is less at night, so watering at evening time is most economical.

242 *Why do some gardeners always water in the mornings?*

In cold, clear weather watering in the morning allows the water, often from the cold tap, to warm up in the soil with the heat of the sun. This is perhaps better than allowing the ground to be wetted just before freezing night temperatures.

243 *How much of the water we give plants is actually used up by them?*

Of every 1000 gal of water taken up by plants in your garden only 2–3 gal will be absorbed by the plant.

244 *Why is it sometimes said that watering should not be done in sunshine?*

If you splash the leaves the drops of water may concentrate the sun's rays to burn their surfaces. In addition, the water speeds up evaporation from the leaves and so actually increases the plant's water demand. However these comments apply mainly to hot mid-day sun. Many rapid-growing plants benefit from top spraying at other times.

245 *What causes plants to wilt in dry weather?*

Plants don't have bones like animals. The stiffness of their stems and leaves is caused entirely by the internal pressure of liquid within their cells, blowing them out like balloons. They remain stiff only so long as they contain water under pressure. Shortage of water causes this interior pressure to drop and the leaves collapse like punctured tyres.

246 *How can I prevent mosquitoes breeding in the water I store in my garden?*

If the butt can be emptied from below by a tap or other means, try pouring a teaspoonful of paraffin on to the surface of the water. This covers it completely sealing the surface and preventing the mosquito larvae from getting air. The water below is not affected.

247 *As soon as the weather becomes really hot the local authorities prevent watering from domestic supplies – how can I deal with this problem?*

The traditional gardener used to collect rain water in barrels. These are no longer easily obtained and you may be tempted to buy large oil drums. Unfortunately, there is no easy way of completely cleaning these of oil residues. Plastic dustbins are cheap and hold a fair amount.

248 *What is mulching?*

Covering the soil with a thick, moist layer of peat, compost, grass clippings or other fibrous, spongy material. This 'mulch' prevents evaporation in hot weather and may be kept moist by spraying. Mulches are not dug in.

249 *Should I apply mulches at other times?*

Apply in late spring, after the sun has warmed the soil to some extent. Water the ground beneath before applying the moistened mulch. This is especially valuable on light soils

4   49

which may dry to powder, or heavy clays which may bake
solid.

250 *Is it true that you can grow plants entirely in water?*

Yes, this is *hydroponics*. Commercially it has been widely
used.

251 *How is plant-growing without soil possible?*

Plants live on chemicals extracted from the soil, so soil itself
is not, strictly speaking, necessary. If you can give the plants
some means of support for holding themselves upright, then
their roots will do just as well in a water solution containing
plant chemicals in the correct proportions.

252 *Surely plants grown like this are very 'artificial'?*

No, there is no difference to the plant, whether it gets its
chemicals from a dilute solution like this or from the soil. In
fact in many cases the plants are healthier, since they are
free from many soil-borne diseases. Often their yield is only
limited by the capacity of the greenhouse and the length of
daylight available.

253 *Presumably this method is mainly used for greenhouse
work?*

Yes, because the complete control of the environment is then
possible: food temperature, aeration and even light. It is also
possible to grow hydroponic plants out of doors.

254 *Can plants be grown in this way by amateurs?*

It makes an interesting experiment, but don't rely on it for
your main crops. The technique requires very meticulous
handling of the chemicals, watering and other factors. For
commercial use it has the advantage of being fairly easily
automated. For amateurs it should just be treated as an
interesting side-line.

Diseases and Pests
255 *What are the best ways to protect vegetables from pest
and disease attack?*

Good cultivation, careful weeding, watering and feeding,
produces plants of the healthiest kind which can resist attack.

256 *What causes plant disease?*

Mainly fungi which include moulds, rots and mildews and viruses. These often show by mottling and distortion of leaves.

257 *How are they dealt with?*

Spray or dust against fungus attack with specially prepared chemicals. Cures for virus diseases are difficult. Remove and burn the affected plants. It is best to buy virus-free seed or plants, or varieties that are immune.

258 *What sorts of fungicides are there to choose from?*

Broadly speaking, most are based on sulphur, copper and certain organic chemicals. In the sections on the vegetables themselves, the common diseases and their treatments are discussed.

259 *Are there any general rules to follow about disease treatments?*

Always follow the makers' instructions precisely. It is most important not to give too strong a spray. It may cure the disease but kill the plant!

260 *I have heard that some sprays taint the fruit or vegetables?*

In such cases you will find that the makers advise not to spray for a period before harvest. The organic chemical BHC can taint the soil, so is not used on root crops. A variety called gamma-BHC (Lindane) must be used for these crops (except potatoes).

261 *Are there any fungicides I can make up at home?*

Bordeaux mixture and Burgundy mixture are both useful, copper-based fungicides.

262 *How can I prepare Bordeaux mixture?*

Buy 1 lb copper sulphate and 1 lb quicklime (wetted slaked lime). Dissolve it (copper sulphate *first*) in 10 gal of cold water. Always prepare it just before use.

263 Is Burgundy mixture similar to Bordeaux mixture?

Yes, but instead of lime use $1\frac{1}{4}$ lb washing soda.

264 What is Cheshunt Compound?

This liquid is used to soak seed boxes just before the seeds are put in. It prevents 'damping off', a fungus that attacks the stems of seedlings. You can buy it ready made.

265 What are the main sulphur-based fungicides?

These may be either lime sulphur, sulphur dust or colloidal sulphur.

266 How do they differ?

Lime sulphur and colloidal sulphur are sprays; sulphur dust is a powder.

267 What are organic fungicides?

They contain chemicals based on carbon and there are many kinds. Thyram or Karathane are useful. Again, study the instructions carefully!

268 Are there as many sprays for insect pests as there are fungicides?

Yes, and these tend to be more poisonous to humans than those for fungi. Most sprays kill both beneficial and harmful insects, so spray as little as possible, and in the evening, when bees, for example, are less active.

269 What are the most important pesticides for the amateur gardener?

Calomel (mercuric chloride) is used as a dust to protect onions and cabbage against the cabbage root fly and to some extent club root in the brassica family. Derris is a natural product which can be used against most of the small insects – greenfly, caterpillars and so on. It is certainly one of the best, since it is not poisonous either to animals or humans. (It does, however, kill fish, so keep it out of any pond.) Pyrethrum is another natural product, safe to use.

270 *There are many chemicals I have heard of with odd names and initials like DDT, Dieldrin, Aldrin, etc. Are all these safe?*

The regulations concerning these types change rapidly, because long-term investigations have shown that many are a hazard to health. Always buy sprays from a professional seedsman who will have up-to-date information on the types which research has proved safe to use.

271 *Are there any chemicals which make plants poisonous to insects?*

Yes, these are known as 'systemic' insecticides. They are absorbed into the plants and when greenfly suck the sap they are poisoned. Those on sale are believed to be safe, but it is very important to keep strictly to the manufacturers' instructions.

272 *Apart from spraying, is there any other help that I can give plants troubled by greenfly?*

Try a fortnightly watering with ½ oz potash nitrate dissolved in a 2 gal can. This is a rapid-acting fertiliser and the spurt of growth seems to make the plant less attractive to aphids.

273 *What are aphids?*

This is the correct name for many tiny pests usually known commonly as greenfly. They also include the blackflies found on broad beans. They live on the leaves and stems of young shoots and can do a lot of damage by causing the leaves to become twisted or the flowers deformed. They are particularly troublesome if plants grow too richly due to heavy fertilising causing a soft, weakly growth.

274 *How do I get rid of aphids?*

They need continual attention because they grow and breed rapidly. Some people spray once and expect this to do for the entire season, or occasionally blame the insecticide if the aphids return. However, they often come back from other plants even after being completely eliminated. Various proprietary preparations are used; apply sprays to both sides of the leaves.

275 *I am reluctant to use poisons of any sort. Is there any way I can reduce insect perils without using them?*

The best approach is to reduce the insect population of your garden.

276 *How can I do this?*

Reduce the number of places where insects can breed by quickly getting rid of fallen leaves and other debris to the compost heap. Make sure that all your plants have adequate food and water. Healthy plants are much less subject to insect attack than weakly ones. Keep weeds down, because these provide additional breeding places for pests.

277 *Though many insects are harmful there must be some which are beneficial. What are the main ones?*

The large ground beetles that run about so quickly hunt pest insects. Ichneumon flies attack caterpillars, whilst centipedes eat many pests that are found in the soil. The hover fly (it looks like a tiny wasp) remains hovering perfectly over flowers and its young feed on aphids. Finally, the familiar ladybird has peculiarly shaped dark grey grubs which also eat greenfly.

278 *What is the difference between millipedes and centipedes?*

The centipede is larger and yellower than the dark millipede. If you get a close look, each joint of the centipede's body has one pair of legs, but millipedes have two pairs of legs to each joint.

279 *What damage does the millipede do?*

It attacks the roots of plants and can spoil germination, or burrow holes into tubers or bulbs. Some gardeners use naphthalene dug into the top few inches of soil in an attempt to eliminate them.

280 *Is it true that worms are a gardener's friend?*

In working their way through the soil millions of worms do much the same job as we do with the spade. They break up the soil, chewing it into small particles and their casts enrich it. There are such vast quantities of worms in fertile land that their efforts are often sufficient alone to keep the soil in good order. Indeed, on grass fields it is common for the weight of worms under the ground to be greater than the weight of cattle on top!

281 Are wasps harmful?

If you have fruit, wasps can be a real trouble, but they do also attack greenfly.

282 How harmful are birds in a vegetable garden?

Most do little harm and may indeed help in keeping down insect pests. It is best to encourage birds in any place where you are not growing either tree or bush fruit. However, they do attack young turnips and radishes and of course peas. You can protect these by laying gossamer threads of glass fibre over them and these are cheaply available.

283 How can I deal with earwigs?

The best plan is to trap them. Cut coarse cloth or sacking into bits about 6 in square and lay them on the ground near their haunts. They hide under the sacking during the day and it is easy to catch them.

284 What are the grey, fat grubs, rather like caterpillars, which I find when digging my garden?

Destroy these as they are probably cockchafer grubs which live on the roots of plants. If there are many, you can work a killer dust such as Lindane into the soil.

285 In my soil I have found many inch-long grubs with yellowy, tough skins, but without legs. What are these?

They are probably leatherjackets (the young of the daddy longlegs). These are specially common if you have just dug up your soil from pasture or if the ground is damp. You will find that cultivation itself will cut down numbers and commercial insecticides will remove any that remain.

286 How can I kill slugs?

Metaldehyde is often used to kill slugs. In addition (but less effective) you can use copper sulphate, salt, soot, naphthalene, alum, etc.

287 *Which are best, insecticides and fungus sprays or dusts?*

Dusts are easiest and cheapest to apply because you don't need any apparatus or water, but they are not so permanent. You may have to give 2 treatments of dust for every 1 of spray. To spray effectively you must have a good syringe, thoroughly cleaned after use. Even small traces of poison remaining can be fatal if you use the syringe for other purposes later. Always wear old clothing. Very few sprays are dangerous if you follow makers' instructions.

288 *How can I keep cats out of the vegetable garden?*

This is difficult. You can try pepper, or small bottles sunk to soil level and filled with ammonia. Cats don't like the fumes.

289 *Do moles do any real damage?*

Only the appearance of the ground is disturbed by the mole hills. They feed on many noxious insects.

290 *Can I trap moles without killing them?*

If you can find the main run of the diggings, which is usually 6–12 in below the surface, you can make a 'pot trap'. Scoop off the soil level with the top of the main run. Dig further down and sink a large tin or flower pot about a foot across, arranging it so that the rim is level with the floor of the run. Grease the container sides and drop into it some fresh earthworms. Next, cover the hole with a piece of dirty board, fixed so that it becomes the 'roof' of the run. Lay the soil back on to this board. Moles that fall into the container cannot climb out. Inspect the run every day or two.

291 *Is it true that moles have a great sense of smell?*

Yes; while making these traps it is vital to wear gloves and if possible to have a few drops of aniseed to sprinkle around to conceal the human scent on the trap.

Part 2
A to Z of Garden Vegetables

Angelica
292 *What is angelica and how is it used?*

It is a relative of the parsley and grows up to 6 ft tall. The leaves, midribs and stalks are edible and may be used for flavouring.

293 *How is angelica grown?*

Sow seed in late summer in a position protected from full sun. Thin to about 2 ft apart. The plants develop slowly taking 3 years to flower.

Artichokes
294 *There appear to be several kinds of artichoke. How do they differ?*

The Chinese and Jerusalem artichokes are roots, the Chinese rather twisted and the Jerusalem tubers similar to potatoes. The globe artichoke produces spherical flower heads of closely packed leaves which are cut and eaten steamed or boiled. Although all three are relatively easy to grow, each requires different treatment.

globe
295 *Is the globe artichoke grown much?*

It is more common on the Continent than in Britain. The flower heads have a very distinctive taste and are considered a delicacy. The amount of actual food obtained from each head is quite small. ·

296 *How are the globe type grown?*

You need a deep, well-dug and rich soil. It is usual to grow from plants. These are divisions of older plants put out in March or April, about 2 ft apart and a yard between rows.

297 *Can I grow artichokes from seed?*

This is possible, though not all seed comes true to type. Grow a surplus in case this happens. Sow the seeds in drills outdoors in April, and thin out to 9 in apart. The following spring they will be ready for transplanting.

298 Do globe artichokes need chemical fertilisers?

The best fertiliser is certainly well-rotted stable or farmyard manure applied heavily in May, and lightly forked in. Good compost is also excellent, especially if deeply dug in before planting. Chemical manures should not then be important, but you can give nitrogen-rich kinds two or three times during the growing season.

299 Should I put the plants in shade or sun?

In full sun; certainly nowhere that is likely to be damp. They are only completely hardy on warm, light, dry soil.

300 We live in a cold area, so presumably artichokes need protection in winter?

Yes, they don't like too much frost. Cut down all the flower stems in October. Heap sand or ashes around the plants before the frosts arrive and strew the surface with peat or straw. This can be taken away after the frosts in March and a top dressing of well-rotted manure given shortly afterwards.

301 When can I expect to cut the first heads?

2 full years after planting out.

302 When are the main heads of globe artichokes harvested?

In late summer when they are fully developed, but before the scales open fully. Cut an inch of the stems with each head.

303 What is a chard?

Chards are young stems which develop after the artichoke heads have been cut in July. They are blanched to keep them white by packing straw round the stems and covering them with soil, a process which takes about six weeks. (A chard is also a name used for salsify.) Incidentally, side buds may form below the main artichoke head. Until the main head has been taken, these should be broken off, but afterwards they can be allowed to grow on and picked and eaten steamed or boiled.

304 How exactly do I divide my old plants?

After 2 years cutting, pull off the suckers (side stems with roots attached) in March or April. Plant these after re-digging and manuring the bed and throw away the remainder.

305 What diseases or pests attack the plants?

Greenfly and blackfly are the main problems. Spray with pesticide but avoid the flower heads.

Jerusalem
306 Does the Jerusalem give better value as a vegetable?

It certainly gives greater weight. The plants are very hardy and last all through the winter. However, some people find the tubers, which are without starch, a little coarse.

307 What type of soil do they need?

They will grow in almost any soil which has reasonable drainage but prefer medium or light types. Very rich soil may make them grow too much to leaf and reduce the weight of the tubers.

308 How do they grow?

Anything up to 8 ft tall. They are often planted in a bed across the windward end of a garden to make a windbreak. You can grow them by wire netting to make a really strong screen.

309 How much lime should I give them?

4 oz per sq yd except in alkaline soils.

310 What are their fertiliser needs?

Like most plants, they like a fertile soil, but generally additional chemicals are not needed.

311 How big should the seed tubers be?

About the size of a hen's egg.

312 *How many tubers will I need for a bed of 10 sq yd?*

30, weighing approximately 3 lb.

313 *When and how are the seed tubers planted?*

From January to April, 4 in deep, spaced a foot or so apart
and with 2–3 ft between rows.

314 *When are the artichokes ready for eating?*

In late autumn. Cut the leaves down as they wither in
October or November, but leave the tubers in the ground
through the winter, digging them only as required. If you
must clear the ground, lift and store them under straw and
soil outdoors, like potatoes. Small pieces you leave in place
will grow again, so make a thorough job of clearance.

315 *Why do artichoke tubers blacken as they boil?*

It may be due to using inferior seed. Recently developed
varieties are better.

Chinese
316 *What soil do Chinese artichokes need for best results?*

Sandy and light but fertile. Too rich soil makes the tubers
coarse.

317 *Do they need the same treatment as Jerusalem artichokes?*

Yes, but plant the tubers closer together, in March, 6 in deep
with about 12–18 in between the plants in all directions.
They need a bright position and plenty of water, particularly
during hot summer weather.

318 *When will they be ready for harvest?*

From November to March.

319 *Are they quite hardy?*

In light soil it is safe to leave them over the winter, being dug
as required, but in heavy or damp land, lift and store them.

Asparagus

320 *Is asparagus very difficult to grow?*

It is relatively difficult on clay soil where there is a lot of work needed in preparing the bed.

321 *How is a bed made on heavy land?*

Prepare raised beds, 5ft wide and 6 in or more above the normal soil level by digging out the good topsoil from the side paths. Ideally, make sure of first-class drainage by mixing in rubble at the bottom of the bed. Add plenty of leaf-mould and well-rotted manure. Cover the surface with more well-rotted farmyard manure and carefully fork this in.

322 *Presumably this preparatory work is simpler on light soil?*

Yes; simply choose a place, preferably with a southern aspect, and dig it deeply, mixing in well-decayed farmyard manure. The deeper you go, even up to 4 ft, the better the results. Add a 4 oz per sq yd dressing of bonemeal and a scattering of soot.

323 *I haven't much room for asparagus; can I grow a single row?*

Yes; make up a narrow bed like a ridge and drive stakes in along it. Supporting strings can then be stretched along to hold the tall fronds up. (This prevents them spreading wastefully over neighbouring soil.)

324 *Can I grow the plants from seed?*

Yes, though it takes time. Sow in April 1 in deep and thin to 1 ft apart, ready for planting out the next year. To save time it is better to buy two- or three-year-old crowns. The three-year-olds can be cut lightly the year after planting.

325 *How many asparagus crowns do I need to feed a family of 4?*

About 6 dozen.

326 *I have been told that male asparagus plants are better than female. Is this correct?*

Yes, always order male plants which give a better and heavier crop. Female plants have berries and should be dug out and replaced by males.

327 *Is there any special planting method?*

Make 3 ridges, each 3 in high, along the bed. Place the crowns on top with their root ends spread down on either side, and spaced 18 in apart. Cover them with 3 in of soil.

328 *When is planting done?*

At any time in April. The roots must never be allowed to dry out. Water the bed before and after planting.

329 *What special care do the young plants need?*

Encourage growth by hoeing off weeds. This also aerates the soil and keeps a cool, moist root-run for the plants. At the end of October, cut off all the growth and cover the bed with a thin layer of well-rotted manure. (Seaweed may be used instead of manure.)

330 *Are chemical fertilisers used?*

2 oz superphosphate and 1 oz nitrate of soda per sq yd can be applied in the following spring, and salt at 2–4 oz per sq yd is usually put on in June; a weekly liquid manure feed of 1 oz each superphosphate and nitrate of soda in 2 gal water is needed throughout the growing season.

331 *When can I start cutting?*

Not at all in the first year, and only a little in the following year.

332 *Once the bed is mature, for how long a period can the asparagus be cut?*

From the first shoots reaching 6 in tall until the middle of June. The remaining shoots should be left to grow on and form the familiar tall, feathery foliage. Though very decorative, this must not be cut off. The weaker shoots however can be trimmed.

333 *When picking, should I cut or break the stems?*

Preferably saw them off an inch or more below the soil surface with the serrated edge of an ordinary bread knife. This reduces the bleeding which a clean cut may cause. In general always leave as many stems as you take off.

334 How can I force asparagus for early use?

Take up roots early in the year and put them in a warm frame 4 in deep. Unfortunately, this usually ruins the plants which must be thrown away afterwards.

335 Does the bed need any further attention after June?

This is its period for recovering strength. Continue feeding with liquid manure and a monthly 1 oz dressing of nitrate of soda. Then at the end of October cut off all growth down to soil level and cover the surface with a mulch of farm manure or compost.

336 Can I use any other material for top dressing asparagus beds?

You can use leaf-mould, burnt refuse, finely granulated peat or seaweed. Add 4 oz bonemeal or mixed general fertiliser before applying these.

337 Should I restock asparagus beds every few years with younger plants?

If the bed is cropping well there is no advantage to be gained in disturbing it. Some beds over 25 years old still do well.

338 What is the asparagus beetle?

This has grubs which attack young foliage and stems. They are less troublesome in the south. As soon as damage is noticed use a proprietary insecticide dust or Derris spray.

339 Could you summarise the year's work for asparagus growing?

In winter spread a 2 in mulch of stable manure, compost or seaweed. You can cover this lightly with fertile earth. In early spring, apply 1 oz nitrate of soda, 2 oz superphosphate or 4 oz bone flour. After mid-February cover each crown with 2–3 in of sand or sandy soil. Cutting can start and continue

until the middle of June. During summer, apply a 2 oz salt
dressing and every month give 1 oz of nitrate of soda. Apply
liquid fertilisers fortnightly. After June, allow the foliage to
grow, but cut it all down in late autumn. Apply 4 oz bonemeal, or general garden fertiliser, then lightly fork and top
dress the bed with compost or rotted fertiliser.

Basil

340 *Can the herb basil be grown in this country?*

It is grown as an annual and must be sown under glass in
April. Plant out the seedlings 8–9 in apart in June. They will
be fully grown in August when they can be cut and hung up
in bunches for storage.

Beans

341 *What are the main types of bean grown in our gardens?*

Broad beans, about 18 in high, from which we eat only the
bean itself; runner beans, about 6 ft tall and rapid growing;
the French bean or kidney bean is usually small bush size
though there are climbers too and we eat the whole pod on
these.

342 *Do broad beans do well in small gardens?*

Yes; although they are usually a farm crop, they are simple
to grow at home.

343 *What are the different types?*

3 types are grown: Dwarf, Longpod and Windsor. Long-
pods are better for early sowings, but Windsors give better-
tasting beans.

344 *I don't have very good soil. Will broad beans still grow
there?*

Yes, they are tolerant of most soils, though they do best on
land which has previously grown a well-manured crop such
as potatoes.

345 *Should I give lime?*

Yes, in most cases. The soil must not be too acid (though
beans in general prefer acid to alkaline soils).

346 *Do broad beans need fertilisers?*

There is no need to give organic manures if the land is reasonably fertile. Give phosphates and potash a fortnight before sowing, perhaps by a mixture of 3 parts of super-phosphate, 2 parts of sulphate of potash and 1 part of sul-phate of ammonia, scattered at 2 oz per sq yd. Before autumn sowing try giving 2 oz per yd of basic slag.

347 *When is the main sowing period?*

Sow in March or April. Broad beans are very hardy and you can also plant them during October and November to grow over the winter.

348 *What is the sowing method?*

Simply put the seeds in 2 or 3 in deep and 9 in apart. Arrange the rows in pairs, spaced 10 in apart. Then allow 2 ft 6 in before the next pair of rows. Dwarf sorts can be planted closer, say 6 in apart.

349 *How many broad bean seeds are needed?*

For a crop of 10 lb sow about 8 yd of row, and a pint of seed sows about 10 yd.

350 *Do broad beans need supports like other beans?*

The shorter types do not, but in windy places especially, tall plants can be helped by double strings stretched beside the stems from posts driven in along the rows.

351 *What special cultivation needs have broad beans?*

As the seedlings grow their first few inches earth them up over the lower part of their stems to produce more roots. At maturity, when the flowers cover about 18 in of the stem, pinch the tops off. This helps pods to develop.

352 *Long side shoots are springing from the base of some of my broad bean plants. Should these be left on?*

Remove them right at the bottom.

353 *When will spring-sown beans be ready?*

5

Late summer to autumn.

354 *Can broad beans be forced early?*

Only under glass. Put half a dozen seeds into a large pot in December or January and grow them on. For early plants to put outdoors, sow single beans in pots in February in heat and plant out after the frosts.

355 *What are the chief bean diseases?*

Rust, a fungus disease, produces spots which turn gradually dark brown. There is no effective treatment. Dig up the plants and burn them. Another fungus disease is chocolate spot, more or less described by its name. It may be caused by too wet conditions for winter-grown crops and is found most often where potash is short. Some gardeners use flowers-of-sulphur dusted over, and a dusting of sulphate of potash before sowing might reduce the trouble. Again, it is best to burn the infected plants.

356 *What about pests?*

The only real pest is blackfly. This is often seen on the growing tips of plants in May or June. Pinch out the growing points of the bean-shoots complete with the flies. Then apply Pyrethrum insecticide or soft soap.

French or kidney
357 *Are french beans easy to grow?*

In the south they are one of the simplest of all garden crops, especially if your soil is light and has been well manured the previous season.

358 *Do they need moist or dry conditions?*

On the dry side (but give a surface mulch in mid-summer to save too much water being lost by evaporation).

359 *Do they need protection?*

Beans like warm soil. Stand cloches over the rows for 2 weeks before early sowings and have them ready again to protect the plants from the July sowings.

360 Will the land need fertilisers?

A mix of ½ oz of sulphate of potash and 1½ oz of superphosphate per sq yd will help on sowing.

361 When are the seeds sown?

To avoid a glut at any one time, make 3 or even 4 separate sowings throughout the period April to July.

362 How many dwarf beans do I need per row?

1 pint of beans will sow at least 80 yd. Soak the beans for a day before sowing.

363 What yield is likely from this amount?

On average, assuming they are sown at intervals, a total of 80 yd should yield about 50 lb.

364 How are the beans sown?

They're sown in drills 3–4in deep (some gardeners sow more shallowly) and with 2–3 ft between the rows. As the plants germinate, thin out to about 8 in apart. You can also sow double rows, at closer spacing, down to 6 in apart. Wider-spaced plants often give better quality crops especially if they are picked as soon as they are ripe.

365 I am told that peas and beans should be sown in rows spaced apart to the eventual height of the plants. Surely this is very wasteful of space?

No; these crops definitely need such wide spacing. The ground between can however be used throughout the spring to grow lettuce, turnips, early cauliflowers, etc.

366 When can I expect the first crops?

From late July. Spray overhead with plain water at weekly intervals after plants reach a foot tall. This speeds flower setting.

367 I live in the north and have many times tried to grow dwarf beans without success. Can you suggest a good procedure?

Dwarf beans in the northern half of the country are very variable in results. Maybe you are sowing much too early. Do not sow until the end of May at the earliest. You have to be lucky with the weather too. A wet summer will cause flowers to drop.

368 Can I get earlier beans in any way?

Only by having a warm greenhouse, in which case sow seeds 3 or 4 to a 6 in pot in early March. Grow them on for putting out as soon as weather allows, usually early June.

369 What about getting beans in winter?

They need a warm and humid atmosphere. In a greenhouse you can sow in large pots of John Innes compost, about $\frac{1}{2}$ in deep and about 2 in apart. Make several sowings between September and March. Do not allow the roots to become sodden although the plants must never dry out completely.

370 How can I collect my own seeds ready for the following year?

Leave some later pods until they are fully ripe. Then lift the entire plant and hang, roots upwards, until they are completely withered. The beans can then be removed and stored.

371 What is the difference between the climbing french bean and the runner bean?

Climbing french do not grow so vigorously as the runners and do not grow up poles so neatly. Strictly the scarlet runner bean is a half-hardy perennial whereas the french bean, whether climbing or bush, is a half-hardy annual. However, the french climbing type often crop better than dwarf beans.

372 Are climbing french beans like the dwarf sort?

Yes, in general, but the climbing supports have to be taller.

373 What pests are likely?

Only blackfly, and this is not a great problem. Derris spray can be used.

68

374 *I have seen beans in yellow pods which appear to be cooked whole with the pod. What are these?*

These are probably golden butter beans. They are treated very much like dwarf beans.

375 *What is their sowing time?*

Sow at the end of April in most areas directly outdoors 2 in deep and 3 in apart, with 18 in between rows. Later on, space them out to 1 ft apart.

376 *What are waxpod beans?*

These are beans used like french beans but they are cooked whole instead of being sliced up. The pods have no 'strings'.

377 *Are they easy to grow?*

On light land they are very easy. Make several sowings, from mid-May onwards.

378 *How much seed will I need?*

A pint of seed sows 20 yd. They are put in drills 6 in wide and 2 ft apart, with 6 in between the seeds.

379 *What type of manures will they need?*

On normally fertile land, hardly any is needed, although potash in the form of wood ashes or sulphate of potash is useful.

380 *When will they be ready for use?*

During summer in July and August, depending on the weather.

381 *What are Dutch brown beans?*

These are not much grown but are intended for use like butter beans. When the pods are full the whole plant is dragged up and hung to dry. A few weeks later shake the beans from their pods and store them in glass jars.

382 *Is there any special growing method?*

Use the usual method for cultivation. Sow at the end of May in double rows with the seed 6 in apart and allow 2 ft between the rows. A pint sows about 20 yd.

383 *Do they need fertilisers?*

They do not require nitrogen, but give a mixture of superphosphate and sulphate of potash, as for kidney beans.

Runner
384 *Should I have a special bed for scarlet runner beans?*

Yes, this is usually convenient. They grow happily on the same soil year after year, so you can erect a permanent climing frame for them, with netting and posts.

385 *What soil type is best?*

A light soil but rich in organic plant foods is ideal.

386 *I suppose therefore the soil must be well prepared?*

The soil will need deep digging, with good compost or organic farmyard manure mixed in at the time. Do this the autumn before sowing.

387 *Should I give chemical fertilisers too?*

A mixture of 3 parts superphosphate, 2 parts sulphate of potash and 1 part sulphate of ammonia given at 2 oz per sq yd will do nicely. Some gardeners on fertile land leave out the sulphate of ammonia. Others use mainly bonemeal.

388 *Must I give lime?*

Not always. Runner beans like fairly acid soil. Make a test, if possible.

389 *What about feeding during growth?*

Start in August with nitrate of soda at 1 oz to a 2 gal can, applied every 10 days or so.

390 *When and how are runner beans planted?*

In late April to mid-May, 2–3 in deep. The exact spacing depends on the fertility of the soil, usually about 8 in apart.

Allow at least 6 ft between rows. Or you can grow in double rows 1 ft apart and with 9 in between the seeds, allowing 6 ft between the pairs of rows.

391 *How much seed do I need?*

1 pt sows about 12 yd. Soak them overnight before sowing.

392 *How many beans will I get?*

On average, 10 lb per yd.

393 *Should I erect the climbing poles first?*

Yes. Although by delaying until after germination you can place the poles beside the seedlings, you are likely to damage their roots with the poles or by treading. A seedling that springs up a little way from a pole can easily be trained up to it.

394 *Do I have to tie the stems in place?*

Only at first for after they have reached the poles or netting they will themselves twine in spirals turning opposite to the course of the sun. When they reach the pole tops, pinch off the growing tips of the stems.

395 *How can I prevent the poles being blown down in wind?*

Sow the seeds in double rows about 1 ft apart and insert the stakes outside these rows, leaning inwards. Allow them to cross about 1 ft from their tops and tie them there. Lay a strong, long pole across the tops resting in the V above the ties and lash to every upright pair. Finally, at each end of the row lean the stakes inwards against the ends of this cross pole and tie them securely.

396 *Can I prevent flowers falling from my runner beans, especially after showers?*

You can try spraying overhead with plain water and giving a feed of 1 oz of sulphate of iron in 10 gal of water. (Give about $\frac{1}{2}$ gal for every yard run of each row.) This defect may also be caused by dry conditions or cool nights.

397 Do runners need watering in summer?

Many parts of this country lack adequate water during the
summer and any of the bean or pea family benefit by extra
water in dry weather. Dig very shallow trenches on either
side of the rows and fill these daily with water which will
soak into the ground. You can also spray overhead with a fine
spray. Plants absorb water through leaves as well as roots.
Runners also benefit by having a mulch of compost, leaf-
mould or even grass clippings an inch deep spread over the
surface to prevent drying out.

398 How can I get the biggest crops of runner beans?

Make sure the soil is deeply dug and very fertile. Then try the
'archway' growing method. Sow 2 rows of beans 8 ft apart.
Space the seeds 1 ft apart and train alternate plants straight
up 9 ft poles. The plants between grow up 4 ft poles. From
the tops of the short poles train them diagonally upwards and
inwards on cords, to meet in an arch 9 ft high, between the
2 rows. A suitable framework of poles, wire and string is
needed. The vertical plants crop in the normal way. Those on
shorter poles bend from vertical to diagonal at 4 ft and this
slightly interrupts the flow of the sap. The result is usually
early and heavy fruiting on the lower parts of the plants, as
well as more beans of quality hanging freely down in the
arch.

399 Isn't this method rather wasteful of space?

No; you can interplant between the rows with lettuce, radish
and other short seasonal crops during the period of development.

400 How can I get earlier crops?

Sow under glass in warmth in spring ready to plant out in
late May.

401 I have heard of growing runner beans very short by
pinching them out at 1 ft high. Is this a good method?

It is possible to grow them into bushes in this way, but the
only advantage is that you don't need to provide the poles.
The crop is very much poorer, both in weight and quality,
and the pods badly curled.

402 *Are there special kinds which grow low naturally?*

There are dwarf types which are not climbers and make small bushes about 18 in tall.

403 *What is the best chemical to use against blackfly on beans? I have tried several sorts without success.*

Perhaps you are not getting at the flies sufficiently. The poison does not work unless you can spray over the insects themselves. Contact with wet stems doesn't seem to injure them so much. Nicotine, Derris or Malathion will all kill blackfly.

404 *Can I grow the grocer's 'butter beans'?*

These are from the lima bean and you would find this difficult to grow here.

405 *What about soya beans?*

It is possible to grow these if you have a long sunny summer. They are sown in May, $\frac{1}{2}$ in deep and 6 in apart. Don't rely on getting a crop though; the weather is a critical factor.

Beetroot
406 *There appear to be three kinds of beetroot; globe, tankard and long-rooted. Which of these are best?*

Globe are best for earlies. The other two are good main crops.

407 *Can the globe or 'turnip' type be used for main crops?*

Yes, in shallow or poor soil. In better conditions the long-rooted type gives heavier, later crops.

408 *What type of soil does beetroot prefer?*

On the light side, and deeply trenched. Like nearly all root crops, beet needs a soil which has not been recently manured (which tends to cause roots to fork).

409 *Does this mean no chemical fertilisers either?*

A dressing of mixed general fertiliser a week or two before sowings will certainly help. Lime will also be needed on most soils.

410 *What crop can beetroot most suitably follow?*

One good crop is leeks, for which the ground will have been deeply prepared and trenched.

411 *What is the seeding season?*

Sow from mid-April for the early globe, through to June for later crops. Sow a little seed each fortnight or month to ensure a regular supply of tasty, medium-sized roots.

412 *How much seed should I buy?*

1 oz of seed sows 50–60 yd.

413 *How is beet seed sown?*

Soak it for a day before sowing. Sow seeds in pairs 1½ in deep and spaced 4 in apart (if grown for salads) or 6 in apart (for the main crop). Select the best seedlings as they develop till the remainder are 15 in apart. Leave 15 in between the rows. You should get 2–3 lb of beet per yd of row.

414 *When will they be ready for lifting?*

Full maturity takes 16–18 weeks, so lift from July onwards. Small beet, suitable for salads, are obtainable after 12 weeks. Fortunately diseases and pests are rarely troublesome.

415 *How can I prevent beetroot 'bleeding' on lifting?*

Twist and break the leaves off instead of cutting them and never wash a beetroot before storage. Store them dry.

416 *Do bruised ones keep satisfactorily?*

No; bruised beet should be used at once.

417 *What storage method is best?*

Lay them out of doors on and under a straw covering with a final topping of soil. Indoors, bed them in dry sand in any cool but frost-proof place.

418 *How long will stored beet last?*

If you check them occasionally for damage and rot, they should last through the winter until the following April.

419 *I have some beet seeds left over from last season. Can I sow them successfully?*

Yes, beet seed will germinate even when it is 8–10 years old.

420 *How can I get early beetroot?*

If you have a warm frame, sow turnip-rooted types from the beginning of January to the end of March. Outdoor sowings in warm areas can be made from mid-March to April.

421 *What is seakale beet?*

This is a beet type, grown not for roots but for green leaves with thick, fleshy midribs. They are grown like beetroot.

422 *Is it true that salt can improve a beetroot crop?*

Yes, dust it along the drills when planting and sprinkle it between the plants in summer.

Borage
423 *How do I grow the herb borage?*

This is quite a large annual plant, but it is fairly easy to raise from seed in spring. It will do well in almost any soil. Sow in rows 15 in apart. Thin the plants to about 1 ft apart later.

424 *Is there a perennial borage?*

This is borage *Borago laxiflora*, but it is a flowering plant, not a herb.

Broccoli
425 *Gardeners often refer to brassicas. What are they?*

Brassicas is the general name for all the cabbage, swede and turnip relatives – broccoli, brussels sprouts, cabbage, cauliflower, colewort, kohl-rabi, savoy, swede, turnip, radish, etc.

426 *Are there different types of broccoli?*

All the different broccoli (and cauliflowers) are much the same plants, though they come to maturity at different times. In general, broccoli may be *sprouting*, with many small heads on side shoots, or *heading* with flower heads like cauliflowers, but smaller. All broccoli are hardy. The sprouting kinds may be white, green or purple.

427 What is the main difference between broccoli and cauliflower?

Cauliflower are ready from August to October, when broccoli are not available.

428 Before planting broccoli is it correct to tread the ground hard?

Like winter cauliflower, the hardy broccoli much prefers to live in firm ground. The firmly packed soil around the roots slows the development of leaves and makes stems and flower heads hard.

429 How do I prepare the soil?

Broccoli grows best following a crop such as potatoes, for which the soil has been deeply dug the previous season. Do not re-dig the seedbed deeply. Lightly fork and rake down the surface and make drills $\frac{1}{2}$ in deep and a foot apart. A dressing of soot helps after seeding.

430 When is broccoli sown?

Winter varieties in March to mid-April for harvest a year later. Early spring varieties in May.

431 How much seed is required?

A $\frac{1}{4}$ oz of seed will sow 20 yd and produce up to 500 plants!

432 What is the final spacing for the plants after transplanting?

Transplant to $2\frac{1}{2}$ ft apart. As with brussels sprouts, and maincrop cauliflowers, they benefit from having plenty of space if you can spare it.

433 Does the crop require watering?

The broccoli and cauliflower group all need plenty of water and an occasional liquid manure during their growing period.

434 How do you harvest broccoli?

Cut the large central head in late summer. Shoots will then develop from the lower joints which can themselves be cut at about 6 in long.

435 Is broccoli hardy right through the winter?

In northern areas winter plants are best covered with a light protection of straw or other litter. It also helps to bend the plants over so that their heads face north before the winter starts. This slows the root action and hardens up the leaves. Earthing up round the stems is an alternative to keep the plants stable in windy parts.

436 Would it not be better to lift and store them?

This is possible, for short periods. Lift them in January and hang the plants upside down in a shed. They will keep for several weeks.

437 What is the best manure for broccoli?

Dressings of well-rotted compost are always good. This can be dug in shallowly or spread thickly over the surface. A top dressing of 5 parts hoof and horn meal, 4 parts superphosphate and 2 parts sulphate of potash at about 4 oz per sq yd will also help to produce large crops.

438 Is lime essential?

Yes; never allow the soil to become acid. Moreover, lime discourages the fungus which causes club root.

439 What is club root?

This is a disease which causes the central root to swell and become abnormally shaped. Prevention is more important than cure.

440 How can I combat it?

Good drainage prevents the damp conditions which favour the fungus. Proper rotation helps (brassica crops should never follow each other on the same ground). Lime does not cure club root but it does reduce the likelihood of it occurring if it is generously applied, making a nearly neutral soil (pH 7.0 or a little less). Another precaution is to put 1 tea-spoonful of mercuric chloride into each planting hole when transplanting. Alternatively, try calomel paste. Mix 1 lb calomel dust to a thin paste with about $\frac{1}{2}$ pt water and coat the roots by dipping them into it before planting.

441 What other diseases attack broccoli?

Other fungi cause ring spot (brown rings on the leaves), downy mildew, white blister and brown mould. These are more or less self-descriptive. Although sometimes prevalent in wet seasons in the south, they are rarely very serious.

442 How can I prevent cabbage butterflies attacking the leaves?

Cabbage white caterpillars can be controlled by many types of modern spray, especially those containing phosphates.

443 What about other pests?

The flea beetle attacks the seedlings and the cabbage root fly lays its eggs in April near the stems, the maggots then feeding on the roots. These can be controlled by using calomel dust in April. The turnip weevil causes round growths (galls) on the roots which are hollow but contain one or more grubs. If these are found when you harvest the plants, make sure that the galls are burnt.

Brussels Sprouts
444 What is the secret of growing brussels sprouts success-fully?

Different varieties of brussels sprouts succeed in different areas. Get the advice of your local seedsman on the variety to choose for your garden. Give plenty of space. Brussels need room for their powerful roots to spread.

445 Which are best, the large or dwarf growing types?

Speaking broadly, the large, strong growing kinds should be grown on poor or medium quality soil, the dwarf varieties on rich soils. The rich feeding available compensates for their dwarf size and the plants do not overgrow themselves. Hybrid varieties often do extremely well.

446 What type of soil preparation is needed?

Like the rest of the brassica group, they like a firm soil which has none the less been deeply dug and manured for a previous crop. They are also responsive to old farmyard manure and good compost dug into the top few inches in autumn (not near planting time). As a top dressing nearer planting, give 5 parts hoof and horn meal, 4 parts superphosphate and 2 parts sulphate of potash at up to $\frac{1}{4}$ lb per sq yd.

447 Is acid soil bad for brussels?

Yes; all the cabbage family prefer to have a fairly limey soil. Measure the acidity and if this is less than pH 6.0 give lime.

448 Is it best to sow seed or buy plants?

In small gardens growing from seed is hardly worthwhile since the plants themselves are usually cheap and not many are needed.

449 When is seed sown?

Sow in mid-March, shallowly, and in rows about a foot apart. They will be ready to transplant in June. For earlier plantings you have to sow in autumn and carry the seedlings through winter in cloches or a cold frame. This is not usually worth the trouble.

450 How much seed is needed?

$\frac{1}{4}$ oz sows 20 yd of drill, giving hundreds of plants.

451 What spacing should I give the plants on transplanting?

In early April put them about 8 in apart to grow on and then in May transplant a second time up to 3 ft apart. Brussels do best with plenty of space.

452 Can I use the space between?

Lettuce or other rapid-growing brassicas can be sown and harvested before the brussels need all the room.

453 Do the plants need watering and feeding?

Always water regularly if there is chance of shortage. Feed lightly with nitrogen until August (no later).

454 *Is there any other way of encouraging good sprout crops?*

Cut back the lower leaves in autumn, but leave the tops intact. When the land is cleared, these can be cut and used as a vegetable.

455 *How can I protect the brussels against wind?*

This is a fairly common problem and can sometimes be helped by earthing up the plants in their early stages. Provide a wind break of matting for example or shelter them by planting behind a northern hedge. You can even put in individual stakes and tie the sprouts to them!

456 *Some of my brussels sprouts' leaves are turning yellow. Is this a disease?*

Probably not, but such leaves should be removed or the leaves nearby may rot.

457 *When can I start harvesting sprouts?*

Pick from October onwards, always from the bottom upwards, and don't cut off the leafy head till all the sprouts are gone.

458 *Why are my sprouts open, instead of solid?*

Loose soil, over-manured at planting may be the trouble.

459 *What are the main problems of brussels sprouts?*

Probably the cabbage white butterfly caterpillars are the most troublesome. Flea beetle can be serious too. Dust with Derris or other proprietary insecticides. Club root attack may take place, as with all brassicas.

Cabbage
460 *What sort of soil do cabbages need?*

Cabbages require plenty of food and the soil must be firm and of good quality.

461 *I suppose this means they need plenty of manure?*

Yes, but it is best to avoid heavy dressings of rich farmyard manures at planting time as this often results in a soft growth of the leaves. It is better to dig the ground deeply some months earlier, adding the manure then, followed after a month or two with a 3–4 oz per yd dressing of lime. The growing plants also need feeding with nitrogen.

462 *How do I apply nitrogen?*

In early spring, apply a top dressing of nitro chalk, sulphate of ammonia, or nitrate of soda at about 1 oz per sq yd. Repeat at monthly intervals through the growing season until August.

463 *How should light soil be prepared for cabbage?*

Use organic manure. This is farmyard manure, compost, etc., dug in during winter. Light soils tend to lose their chemicals more rapidly than heavy types, so give a dressing made with 4 parts hoof and horn meal, 2 parts superphosphate and 1 part sulphate of potash at about 4 oz per sq yd.

464 *On heavy land, after manuring, does cabbage need additional fertilisers?*

A mixed general fertiliser at 2 oz per sq yd is of benefit just before planting.

465 *Does winter cabbage need any fertiliser?*

A 1 oz per sq yd fortnightly dressing of nitrogen helps in showery weather in January and February, but don't sprinkle it on the leaves.

466 *How do I sow seeds for cabbage?*

Sow spring cabbage in July or August on a fine seed bed. Drill the seed very thinly, ½ in deep. Transplant these seedlings in late September or October about 18 in apart. For early summer cabbage, sow in a cold frame in February and put these out in April. For late summer, use a sowing made in March of quick-growing types which will be ready in August. In favoured areas sowings of these sorts, even as late as July, will give some produce before winter. Some gardeners space these 6 in further apart than earlier kinds.

467 *How do I grow pickling red cabbage?*

Seed is sown in August for over-wintering like ordinary cabbage. You can also sow in March for late summer use.

468 *Do the seed beds themselves require fertilisers?*

There should be no fresh manures dug into the seed beds, but a dusting of lime or soot during growth often helps.

469 *How many plants will I get from 1 oz of seed?*

Too many! An ounce will produce up to 700 plants.

470 *Should I dig the ground over before setting out the plants?*

No; it is best to leave the ground undug, simply raking it level and putting them firmly into place. Cabbage do not do well on recently dug ground.

471 *What about watering cabbage?*

For maximum growth of any leafy plant, water supplies must be maintained liberally, especially in warm weather.

472 *Why did my autumn cabbage crop fail which I sowed in May?*

Probably your soil was not quite rich enough. Autumn cabbage requires richer soil than spring types.

473 *Is it correct to leave the main outer leaves in place on the stalks when I remove a cabbage head?*

If you leave the main outer leaves in position shoots will eventually grow up from the plant and make a useful winter green vegetable.

474 *What is the reason for slashing a cross in the top of the cut stalk?*

It encourages the shoot buds to develop.

475 *What are the main diseases of cabbage?*

The most serious is club root. (See broccoli.)

476 *The roots of my cabbage are swollen and hollow. Is this club root?*

No; what you have is probably an attack by the cabbage gall weevil. Club root gives solid swellings with a pronounced smell.

477 *Some of my developing cabbage plants have suddenly wilted, even though the growing conditions appear to be good. What could cause this?*

This is probably an attack by the cabbage root fly.

478 *What protection is there against this?*

There are insecticide dusts to prevent the cabbage root fly and the cabbage gall weevil, which are sprinkled round the base of the young plants as they are put out.

Cardoon
479 *What is a cardoon?*

This is a plant grown for use in stews and soups. It looks and grows somewhat like celery.

480 *Is it grown from seed?*

Yes; sow outdoors in late April, 3 in deep and transplant the seedlings in June 1½ ft apart in trenches, or in rows 2½ ft apart.

481 *Will ¼ oz of seed be enough?*

You will get about 80 plants from this amount.

482 *What sort of soil is needed?*

Cardoon needs plenty of depth and soil as rich as is conveniently possible.

483 *How is the cardoon blanched?*

Wrap hay or straw round the developing stems to within about a foot of the top. Then earth up around them.

484 *When will they be ready for use?*

They will be blanched about a month after being covered.

Carrots
485 *Is it true that carrots only grow on light soil?*

The long-pointed varieties of carrots do undoubtedly grow best on very deep, light soil, but you can still grow carrots of different varieties on any soil.

486 *How do I choose varieties for different soils?*

The lighter and deeper the soil, the longer rooted the varieties to use. For shallow or heavy land, choose short-rooted sorts. These also mature more rapidly, so are best for main crops; long-rooted are best for showing.

487 *How could I improve a heavy soil for carrots?*

Sand, peat and wood ash will all help to lighten the soil and you can also build it up into 1 ft ridges to improve the soil depth and drainage.

488 *Is stony land bad for carrots?*

Yes; stones tend to make roots bend and fork. Dig out the stones along the carrot row while preparing the seed bed.

489 *I suppose deep digging is essential for carrots?*

This depends on the variety. All the long-rooted types must have deep digging, but for short-rooted varieties a single spade depth is adequate, though digging must be thoroughly done.

490 *What about manuring?*

Most gardeners never give organic farmyard or horse manure before planting. This may cause some of the roots to branch. Instead, they rely on old manure dug in deeply several months beforehand for previous crops.

491 *From this answer it sounds as if some gardeners do dig in manures. What is the result?*

By enriching the soil with rotted manure or rich compost,

you get a higher proportion of split or forked roots, but the overall weight of crop is often much greater. This compensates for the poorer shapes.

492 *Are chemical fertilisers needed?*

3 oz per sq yd of mixed fertiliser before sowing is enough and some gardeners use weekly dressings of soot. Others on light land prefer to give a monthly general mixed fertiliser, watered in during dry spells, though too much nitrogen can cause roots to split.

493 *Do carrots grow in shade?*

Yes, provided it is not too dark. Put early sorts in the sun, though.

494 *How much seed will I need to sow a 50 yd row and how much is the crop likely to weigh?*

1 oz seed for 50 yd of maincrop would yield about a hundredweight.

495 *Carrot seed is very small. How deeply should it be buried?*

Sow very shallowly indeed. Simply sprinkle it lightly and press gently down. Some gardeners use wood ash lightly along very shallow drills and also dress the seedlings with soot.

496 *What is the best time for sowing?*

Early sowing time outdoors is February in favoured areas and on a warm, south-facing border or under cloches. In most places though it is better to leave it for a week or two, preparing the ground in March and perhaps sowing in the first weeks of April. Main crops are sown in May or early June and will be ready by October.

497 *How far apart should the rows be?*

You can either sow 9 in apart or you can sow broadcast. The rapid-growing leaves then suppress weeds. Gradually thin out to 6–7 in apart all ways.

498 *When is thinning done?*

When they are 3 in high, plants in rows can be thinned out to 2 in apart, and later to about 7 in apart. The ones removed can of course be used for salads. Remember in any case when thinning carrots to firm the soil back around the remaining plants. Exposed carrot root is subject to attack by the carrot fly.

499 *I have a friend who mixes carrot and radish seed together; is this satisfactory?*

Yes; the radishes grow quickly and can soon be pulled, leaving the carrots spaced out. This is good for a very small vegetable garden.

500 *The tops of my carrots tend to turn green; how can I prevent this?*

Simply earth up the plants lightly to keep the tops covered with soil. Do this early before they turn green.

501 *How can I grow the best possible carrots?*

Use a dibber to make holes spaced 9–12 in apart and roughly 18 in deep. Fill these with very fine, sandy loam and plant 2 seeds in each. Weed out the weakest of the 2 seedlings and keep soot and lime scattered around the rows as the plants grow. Make sure that the soil is open and moist at all times.

502 *When are carrots lifted?*

Before the ground becomes soaked in autumn and early winter. Store them packed in sand.

503 *What pests attack the carrot?*

Only carrot fly is dangerous and commercial sprays can control this. Naphthalene is often used, dusted between the rows at 2 oz per sq yd. Repeat this at 2-weekly intervals through May and June.

Cauliflower
504 *How can I grow a succession of cauliflowers throughout the year?*

Broccoli are better for the cold season, but you can get a long season of cauliflowers. There are 3 main planting times. In February or early March in a frame; early in April outdoors; and the middle of August, also outdoors, to grow through the winter in frames.

505 *What type of soil do cauliflowers need?*

As with most leafy-crops, a rich, deep, moderately heavy soil, which has been deeply dug and manured, especially with nitrogen fertilisers or farmyard manure, gives best results. The ground must also be firm.

506 *How much lime will be required?*

Always keep the lime content up in soil growing cauliflowers (or indeed any of the cabbage family). They need a nearly neutral soil. The pH must never be lower than 6.0. Lime also restricts the development of club root disease.

507 *When are cauliflowers planted out?*

Frame-sown types in April; early outdoor sowings in May or June; later outdoor sowings in September or early October. These last are best left under glass frames or cloches till the following April, when they can be finally moved outdoors to heart up.

508 *How deeply should I sow the seed?*

Sow only ½ in deep, and thinly. Crowded plants are weakened.

509 *Is one transplanting enough for cauliflowers?*

If the seedbed thickens too rapidly you can initially transplant to 9 in apart to grow on. The final spacing, from 2–3 ft apart, depends on the variety.

510 *How big should the transplants be?*

Small plants are best, with no more than 3 leaves. If left to grow bigger, the final crop heads are small.

511 *If I buy seedlings, how should I select and plant them?*

Choose short and sturdy ones, up to 4–5 in tall. Plant them right up to their leaves. Otherwise they tend to develop weak stems which will not support the heavy heads. Showery weather is ideal.

512 *Are liquid fertilisers beneficial?*

Nitrogen fertilisers are good, whether powder or liquid, when the plants are in full growth.

513 *Should I mulch cauliflowers?*

Cauliflowers, more than most of the cabbage group, dislike hot, dry conditions. A thick scattering of moist litter, compost or peat over the surface helps.

514 *When are the heads ready for cutting?*

Cut from April to October from spring sowings. You may need to support the heavy heads by earthing up, or even with stakes, in windy places.

515 *Do cauliflowers need special treatment in winter?*

As cauliflowers heart late in autumn they can be shielded by bending the largest leaves over to cover the hearts, tying them into place if necessary. This bleaches the heads (curds). They may also need water at this time if the summer has been dry.

516 *Why do some of my cauliflowers grow tall and thin?*

This is 'bolting', often caused by too loose soil with little water-retaining capacity. Next time, give farm manure or compost and tread well long before planting out.

517 *Why do some cauliflowers never grow hearts?*

There is a tendency for a few plants to go 'blind' without a flower. Inspect your rows of seedlings to make sure they all have flower buds and remove those without.

518 *Can cauliflowers be stored successfully?*

Flowered plants can certainly be dug up with plenty of earth about their roots and 'heeled in' on a light, sandy soil. Give protection from frost till they are used.

Celeriac

519 *What is the turnip-rooted celery?*

This is another name for celeriac, a useful but none too common vegetable. It develops a swollen, onion-shaped root which can be baked. It throws up leafy sprouts which look like celery but are too bitter to eat.

520 *Is it easy to grow?*

Yes, it does not need quite such rich ground as celery and will do well in any cultivated soil.

521 *Is it better to use fertilisers or organic manures?*

Plenty of rotted farmyard manure and bonemeal at 4 oz per sq yd before putting out the plants is ideal.

522 *Can I grow celeriac from seed?*

Yes, if you have a warm frame. Seeds are sown in March, then pricked out early into boxes or 3 in pots.

523 *The seed seems small. Is $\frac{1}{4}$ oz enough?*

This will do for 2–3 years producing several hundred seedlings!

524 *When are the seedlings put outdoors?*

In May or June, into ground which has been trodden firm after careful digging.

525 *What spacing should I give to the plants?*

Plant them shallowly, 12–15 in apart and with 18 in between rows.

526 *Is celeriac ever earthed up like celery?*

Not at all. In fact, unless you prefer blanched roots, it is better to slowly remove the soil from around the sides of the thickened bulbs at the base of the stems. They then look like onions, standing on the soil.

527 *Are they sensitive to drought?*

They need plenty of water, especially in summer, and it is best to mulch the surface with moist leaf-mould or peat.

528 *Are all the leaf stalks left on?*

Remove those on the sides but leave those at the top.

529 *When are they ready to lift?*

At the year end, November to January.

530 *How much crop will I get?*

A 10 yd row yields about 25 lb.

531 *Can they be stored for later?*

Yes; pack in dry sand. In warmer areas you can also leave them without lifting, covered with straw.

Celery

532 *What types of celery are there?*

White or pink sorts, best grown in trenches and blanched by earthing up, and 'self-blanching' which are planted on flat land 9 in apart. Their leaves then shade and help blanch the stems.

533 *How is celery fitted in with the rotation plan?*

It can follow peas or broad beans.

534 *I have tried to grow celery from seed but the small plants grow far too slowly. Do they need special treatment?*

Celery does grow very slowly in its early stages; this is why the usual sowings are made so early, in February and April in a warm greenhouse or frame. Afterwards you can put the seedlings out into deep boxes or a 'growing-on-bed' of fine soil outdoors, with manure beneath and covered by a cloche or frame. Seedlings will then be ready for transplanting out in May, June or July.

535 *What method is used for seeding?*

Apply a compost mixture of light soil, leaf-mould or peat,

finely sieved. Sprinkle the seeds over the surface, and sieve a thin covering of more fine soil on top. They need a temperature of 16°C (60°F) to germinate satisfactorily.

536 *How much seed is needed?*

Use $\frac{1}{4}$ oz to 20 yd of row. This will give a crop of about 75 lb.

537 *What cultivation should I give the soil?*

Celery will often fail unless it has deep cultivation. It is also a useful crop for a completely new garden where deep digging is essential in any case, but where the soil may not yet be in good condition.

538 *What are celery 'trenches'?*

Deeply dug, narrow beds sunk below the ground level. They make it easier to provide the heavy watering and liquid manuring needed to get good quality crops and also make for less work in earthing up for blanching. Preparation of trenches takes time, but the soil benefits long after the celery has been harvested.

539 *How can I prepare these trenches?*

Deep dig the ground by double-digging. Then take out a trench 8 in deep and 18 in wide. (If only 1 row of plants is wanted, 1 ft wide is enough.) Dig a several-inch thickness of well-decayed manure into the bottom of the trench, and then skim this over with 2–3 in of fine topsoil. The final depth should then be 4 in. Finally soak the trench with water before planting (unless rain has fallen within the last 24 hours).

540 *This will leave ridges on either side. Can I use these?*

Put in catch crops of salads, lettuce etc. They will be gone before the soil is needed for earthing.

541 *What spacing do the plants need in the trench?*

Plant them 8 in apart in 2 rows 1 ft apart. Trenches must be 3 ft apart.

542 *Are later fertilisers needed?*

The original digging in of stable manure and general fertiliser gives a basic fertility on which the celery can draw.
Ammonium sulphate is sometimes given before planting, at
the rate of about ½ oz per sq yd, or 2 oz of general fertiliser,
if manure is short. Liquid manure at fortnightly intervals also
helps.

543 *What other cultivation does celery need?*

Shade the young plants from hot sunshine and give frequent
soakings with water and a weak liquid manure. They must
have plenty of moisture or they may run to seed. This is all
that is really necessary until the time for blanching.

544 *What should I do with stems thrown out separately from the main bunch?*

These are suckers. Cut them off below soil level.

545 *How is white or red celery blanched?*

Start by wrapping brown paper loosely round the young
stems. Then pull the stems together and tie them. Earth up
the sides to about half way and add more in stages to finish
earthing fully by October.

546 *When is celery ready to eat?*

After the first frosts of autumn.

547 *What diseases can be troublesome to celery?*

Leaf spot is the worst problem. The small brown spots can
eventually destroy the whole plant. First-class seed is the best
prevention, together with a routine spraying throughout the
growing period with either a copper fungicide or one such
as Bordeaux mixture.

548 *Why have the insides of my celery plants partially rotted away?*

There are a number of possibilities. Usually this happens in
a wet season, because the growth never becomes hard and
crisp. Other causes are too much nitrogen compared with
potash, or even careless earthing which has forced soil down

into the stems. Bacteria gets into damaged or softened tissues quite easily.

549 *What is the cause of curious pale channels on the leaves in irregular whorls like small tunnels?*

This is caused by the celery fly which feeds on the leaf itself. Try a nicotine spray.

Chervil
550 *Is chervil difficult to grow?*

In any normal soil you can get a crop within a few weeks, from sowings made outdoors in spring.

551 *Is there any special procedure for growing chervil in northern areas?*

Try mixing the seed with about 5 times its own weight of fine, sandy soil in late autumn. Lay the mix in a box in a dry place in winter. Then in February spread the mixture in drills. This long winter rest in contact with soil often improves germination.

552 *Does chervil need protection against frost?*

It is rather tender and you can shield the young plants with polythene, bracken, etc. They should end up about 6 in apart.

Chicory
553 *Can you suggest salads which can be grown for winter, especially in the north?*

Chicory when blanched makes an excellent salad.

554 *Surely chicory is grown through the summer?*

Yes; sow it late in May or very early June in rows 1 ft apart with 9 in between the plants after thinning. The trick for winter use though is to lift these plants in October (after taking off the leaves) and put them into a shed. These are then forced during the winter a few at a time.

555 *How is this forcing done?*

Anywhere warm 13°C (55°F) and totally dark. Take a

batch of roots and place them in boxes of good soil, and cover the crowns, which should be just above the surface, with soft sand, tins or pots so as to keep them completely in the dark. This will blanch the leaves as they grow and these can be cut off to soil level when they reach 6–8 in high.

556 *Do I plant the whole of the thick root?*

It is common to cut away the bottom half of the roots to save space.

Chinese Cabbage
557 *What is Chinese cabbage?*

It is a vegetable rather like a long-leaved lettuce. Another name for it is pe-tsai.

558 *How is it grown?*

It is grown like lettuce. It is not hardy and only thrives in warm areas.

Chives
559 *Are chives difficult to grow?*

No; they grow easily in the sun and any normal soil. They have a mild onion flavour and are used in salads, sauces and with cooked vegetables.

560 *I know that mature chives can be divided and spaced out to grow on, but how do I get the initial batch?*

In March, sow seed in drills 8 in apart, thinning out to about 4 in between the plants. These can be left in place until they mature when they can be divided and spaced a little further apart.

561 *When do I divide chives?*

You can start in January, planting them out 4 in apart. Choose the best bulbs for this, using up the smaller ones.

562 *Can I get chives in winter?*

Yes; dig up a clump in autumn and put it in a pot of compost. Keep on a warmish window sill.

Chou de Burghley
563 *What is Chou de Burghley?*

It is a cross between cabbage and broccoli. Treat it like ordinary cabbage. The cabbage-like leaves can be cut in autumn but if you leave it a flower heart will develop, rather like broccoli, by the following spring.

564 *When are the seeds put in?*

Either in warmth in March for autumn cutting or outdoors in May. The mature plant in spring looks like a small cauliflower surrounded by plenty of cabbage leaves.

Colewort
565 *What is colewort?*

Another name is collard. They are small winter cabbage which never make good hearts, but are useful because they can be grown very closely spaced and can be inter-planted amongst the rows of slower-growing brassicas such as brussels sprouts. They are cultivated like ordinary cabbage.

566 *What season will they be ready for use?*

Autumn and winter, from late spring sowings.

567 *When are coleworts seeded?*

You usually sow seed from April to June, but you can sow in late July and transplant out in September.

568 *What spacing is given to the plants?*

There are dwarf (rosette) and tall kinds. The dwarf are spaced 12–15 in apart, but the tall up to $2\frac{1}{2}$ ft apart.

569 *Are any varieties more suitable than others for winter use?*

Yes, it is best to ask for hardy types for late sowing.

Corn Salad
570 *I have been told of a plant called lamb's lettuce, useful for spring salads. What is its correct name and how is it grown?*

This is corn salad and needs very good drainage. Seeds are sown in spring $\frac{3}{4}$ in deep in drills 9 in apart. Later on, thin the seedlings out to 6 in apart.

Couve Trouchuda

571 *Does couve trouchuda have any other name?*

Yes; portugal cabbage or seakale cabbage.

572 *What is its advantage over ordinary cabbage?*

As well as the cabbage-like heart, you can cook the central stems of the outer leaves in the same way as seakale.

573 *Is it grown like other cabbage?*

Yes, but it is best sown in heat in February to give good plants for putting out in May. Rich soil with lime is needed. Harvest in winter.

574 *What spacing should the plants be given?*

Allow plenty. A yard each way, like brussels sprouts, is not too much.

Cucumber

575 *Can I grow cucumber out of doors?*

There are outdoor 'ridge' cucumbers but much depends upon your area. Cucumbers require long spells of warm conditions for success. In any case they are best started in heat so most gardeners buy the plants ready hardened off for planting out on the ridges.

576 *How can I prepare a cucumber ridge?*

Dig out a trench 9 in deep and about 2 ft wide. Then heap in this enough partly rotted manure of any kind to raise it a foot above the surrounding soil. Replace the soil you have dug out on top so as to leave a flat, raised bed.

577 *Should the ridge be in sun or shade?*

Choose a sunny spot, but not exposed to cold winds.

578 *Can seeds be sown direct?*

Although it is easier to buy plants (which are rarely expensive), you can push groups of 3 seeds 3 ft apart down the centre of the bed and about 1½ in deep. The fruit from these will be a little later.

579 *Is it true that cucumber seeds placed on their sides germinate better?*

Many people believe so and it doesn't do any harm to do it. Stand plant pots upside down over the seeds until germination takes place. The darkness helps them to start. Finally take out all but the strongest plants.

580 *How far apart are the plants put in?*

A yard or more. For small households, 4 plants may be ample.

581 *My outdoor cucumbers grow very rapidly. Indeed, they seem to make far too much growth. Should I control them in any way?*

Yes, it is most important not to allow the plants to grow too vigorously. Select only 3 stems and allow them to grow a yard long (about 6 leaves) before pinching them short.

582 *Is it true that I must remove the male flowers, those without a swollen mini-cucumber below?*

In greenhouses and frames, yes, but ridge types outdoors must be pollinated, so leave all the flowers on.

583 *When should I cut the cucumbers?*

Place slates or plastic under them to keep them from the soil, and cut as early as possible, as soon as they reach a size you can eat. This encourages more to grow.

584 *Will they need feeding or watering?*

Cucumbers must never dry out at the root, and need liquid manures weekly whilst fruiting.

585 *Do pests attack cucumber?*

Greenfly can be a problem. Spray under and over the leaves. A few get virus diseases causing the leaves to become mottled. These plants must be burned.

Dandelion

586 *Can dandelion leaves be eaten as salads?*

Even the ordinary weed kind are edible but you can also buy special large-leaved varieties from some nurserymen either as roots (which can be forced in winter) or as seeds.

587 *They must be easy to grow!*

Drill seed in April and thin till the plants just touch. For winter forcing lift roots and plant in pots or boxes, removing any remaining leaves. Water and keep them warm and dark. New leaves will be blanched and can be picked about six weeks later.

Endive

588 *What can I grow for winter salads?*

Try endive. This is grown like lettuce, but is hardy enough for winter use.

589 *What soil is best?*

A medium, crumbly soil, as for lettuce. Give an ounce of superphosphate before putting in the seed.

590 *How are they sown?*

Sow thinly in April and at intervals until September, in drills 1 in deep and 6 in apart not in shade. Thin out to 1 ft apart later on.

591 *Should they be transplanted?*

Not always, but it is possible where seeds have been started on a separate seed bed. Move them when they are 2 in tall and space them 1 ft apart.

592 *What fertiliser is used?*

Use nitrogen twice whilst growing, dusting nitro chalk along the rows.

593 *Will the plants need protection in winter?*

A little helps. Later sowings are best made in a south-facing, sheltered border. In cold areas, lift some and place in frames (or cover with cloches) in case of loss.

594 *How do I grow endive on heavy land?*

Build up the beds by digging out trenches at the sides 6 in deep so that the ridge in between is flat-topped and about 6 in above normal ground level. This improves the drainage and you can mix in coarse sand to make it better still.

595 *How is endive eaten?*

The leaves are best served raw and blanched, but they can also be cooked.

596 *How is the blanching done?*

Grasp the bunch of leaves together and run a length of raffia or a rubber band around them. (Make sure the plant interior is dry.) The inner leaves will then whiten up in 4–6 weeks. Alternatively, cover the whole plant with a large plant pot with its drain hole blocked.

Fennel
597 *Can I grow new fennel plants from seeds?*

It is best to treat this herb as an annual. Sow in autumn (in warm places) or in April in drills 18 in apart. Move the plants at 4 in high to about a foot apart. The flavour of fennel is reminiscent of anise and the herb is traditionally used to flavour fish or in salads.

598 *I have a perennial fennel plant and I am told that I should cut the flowers off. Is this correct?*

It is usually best to remove flowering stalks for, if they are allowed to develop, they weaken the plant which may die back.

Garlic
599 *We acquired a taste for garlic whilst holidaying abroad. Can it be grown in this country?*

Yes. This is a bulb-like herb. Buy the small 'cloves' and plant them in firm soil to half their depth, 10 in apart all ways, in winter or very early spring.

600 *Will they grow in heavy land?*

They actually prefer a light soil, though they will often succeed in heavy land too. Very light soil must be firmed down, or the young plants may lift themselves out of the soil as the roots extend. Some gardeners plant much deeper, up to 2 in, especially in light land.

601 *How is the crop lifted?*

As the leaves fade, towards the end of July, pull up the plants and hang them to dry in the sun.

602 *Can I save some for future planting out?*

Just pick a few cloves from the edges of the clumps as they are lifted.

Gourd
603 *Can I grow gourds for eating?*

This is possible, but most people prefer the ordinary marrow. Gourds can be started off in April in warmth and put out in June or July. They are treated exactly the same as marrows.

Herbs
These are dealt with individually. For basil, see Q340; borage, see Q423–4; chervil, see Q550–2; chives, see Q559–62; fennel, see Q597–8; marjoram, see Q667–9; mint, see Q696–704; parsley, see Q760–4; sage, see Q873–6; savory, see Q882–4; tarragon, see Q945–6; thyme, see Q947–50.

Horseradish
604 *I have been told not to plant horseradish because it becomes a nuisance. We love the sauce though, so what do you suggest?*

True, horseradish can get out of hand. An old, bottomless tin bath can be used, sunk rim-deep to contain the roots a little.

605 *Since it grows so vigorously, I suppose it is not particular about the soil?*

It grows in most places.

606 *Is horseradish grown from seed?*

This isn't usually necessary because it propagates so rapidly from old plants. Pieces about 6–8 in long can be planted in October about 10 in deep. They are spaced about 1 ft apart with 18 in between the rows.

607 *How should I prepare the bed?*

Deep dig the ground in autumn (this is essential to make good, long roots), but don't mix in much manure apart from very well-rotted compost.

608 *I have been told to make deep holes for horseradish. Does this encourage a good crop?*

It certainly helps to get first-quality roots. The method is straightforward enough. Bore 2 ft deep holes with a dibber made out of an old spade handle, then thrust the crowns of the divided roots down into the holes to the bottom. Don't fill the holes up. The root will in fact fill it up as it grows.

609 *When will they be ready?*

The large varieties will be ready the following November, when you can dig the roots up and store them packed in sand. Small roots will of course be ready earlier.

610 *Are they perennial?*

Yes, in practice, but it is best to clear part of the bed each spring or autumn and replant. In this way there is a constant supply of young growth and the bed's development is kept under control.

Kale (Borecole)
611 *Is kale suitable for a small garden?*

Yes, it gives a very prolific growth of green vegetable right through winter into spring.

612 *Are the plants damaged by frosts when standing out in this way?*

No, kale is very hardy indeed.

613 *What type of soil does it need?*

Ideally, soil should be fairly rich and well cultivated, but firm and in an open position. However kale grows successfully even on poor soils, where other brassicas do badly. After potatoes is a good time, for the soil will have been improved for these by manure and cultivation.

614 *When is kale usually seeded?*

Between March and May, to be ready for planting out in July.

615 *How is the seed sown?*

In a fine seed-bed in 1 in deep drills. As soon as possible, thin the seedlings out to 4 in apart.

616 *For 100 plants, how much seed will I need?*

$\frac{1}{4}$ oz will give up to 750 before thinning.

617 *Are the seedlings much trouble at the transplanting stage?*

No; when they are 6–8 weeks old, space them out with $2\frac{1}{2}$ ft between plants and the same between rows. Water for a week or two after planting.

618 *What about fertilisers for kale?*

If the ground has been well cultivated for an earlier crop its main needs on transplanting will be met by a mix of 2 parts superphosphate to 1 of sulphate of potash. Like all leafy plants, nitrogen is its main need when in full growth. Do not however give nitrogen in the autumn as this weakens winter growth and makes it less hardy. In early spring, after the frosts are largely over, apply nitrogen again.

619 *What is the best variety to use in an exceptionally hard area with severe winters?*

'Hungry gap' is sown in June or July and withstands almost any winter.

620 *Can kale be intercropped?*

You can plant lettuce, carrots or radish between the rows.

621 *How is kale harvested?*

First remove the top part of the plant and use it as a green vegetable. Then as the other shoots grow on, cut them whilst they are still young.

622 *What is asparagus kale?*

This is a variety which produces mainly shoots, rather like asparagus, which are cut for the table. It is sown in June for use in spring.

623 *When and how can I force kale?*

Prepare well in advance. Crowns must be 3 years old before forcing. They can either be forced outdoors or under shelter.

624 *How are forcing crowns prepared most quickly?*

Cut lengths of side-roots in spring, several inches long and bury them completely, 2 ft apart. Reduce the shoots as they appear to one. By autumn they will be ready.

625 *What are the forcing methods?*

Outdoors, heap ashy soil over them in winter, or cover with large pots surrounded by fresh, warm manure. Indoors, pack them in soil-filled boxes in a warm, moist place.

626 *What is Russian kale?*

A variety of kale which produces an autumn heart. If this is left till spring it will develop sprouts rather like sprouting broccoli.

627 *When is it sown?*

April to May. Treat it just like ordinary kale.

Kohl-Rabi
628 *My turnips do badly on my light soil, which dries out in summer. What do you suggest?*

Try kohl-rabi which will withstand quite severe drought. The roots, which are similar to turnip, are best if eaten when only half grown, roughly tennis-ball size. Big ones are tough.

629 *How are they seeded?*

From March to June take out drills only $\frac{1}{4}$ in deep and 15 in between the rows. Thin the plants later to 10 in apart and never transplant them.

630 *Do they need rich soil?*

If following potatoes for instance, they may need no further manuring, just a dressing of 4 oz of superphosphate and 1 oz of sulphate of potash.

631 *How much liquid feeding do they require?*

Feed occasionally during rapid growth.

632 *Can I get autumn supplies?*

For these sow at the end of July or in early August.

Leeks
633 *Is it difficult to grow leeks?*

Leeks are one of the hardiest of all vegetables and can grow outdoors in any part of the country, but the soil must be rich.

634 *Can I start off my own plants from seed?*

Yes; make sowings at intervals in February (with some heat) and between March and May outdoors. Water well the day before sowing unless rain has fallen. Sow quite shallowly with just a bare covering of earth. Transplant in June 8 in apart with 18 in between rows.

635 *How much seed should I buy?*

For 30 yd of row, get about $\frac{1}{2}$ oz.

636 *Is it essential to grow leeks in trenches?*

For the very best exhibition leeks, trenches probably give the best results but for sound-quality household produce there is no need to go to this trouble, especially if your land is not particularly wet. You can grow them on flat beds in holes bored in the ground.

637 *What type of holes do you mean?*

Make yourself a dibber with a round stick about 2 in in diameter. In June, push this into well-prepared ground about 8 in deep, spacing the holes 9 in apart in rows 1 ft apart. Drop the young plants into these holes and pour a handful of fine soil down over their roots. Finally, fill the hole with water. The plants will soon steady themselves and start to grow. Make sure the soil surface doesn't become dry. Keep the hoe moving in the soil.

638 *But surely these holes will gradually fill up as I hoe the ground?*

Yes, gradually, but this is quite satisfactory because it will blanch the developing leeks exactly as they would if grown in trenches.

639 *How are leek trenches prepared?*

In much the same way as for celery. Take out trenches 2 ft apart, 8–10 in wide and at least 1 ft deep. Dig a 3 in layer of well-rotted manure into the bottom. Heap up the soil you take out between the trenches to be used later for earthing up. In June, set the plants down the middle of the trenches 18 in apart. As they develop use the soil to gradually earth them up. Extra early blanching can be given by wrapping cardboard collars around the leaves as they grow.

640 *Isn't it possible to grow leeks on the flat without holes or trenches?*

They do not make such good specimen plants as by the other methods. Take out drills 6 in deep and 18–24 in apart and set plants 8–12 in apart along them. This method is only suitable for ground that is really rich and on the heavy side.

641 *What fertilisers should be used?*

2 weeks after planting out, give 1 oz of superphosphate and $\frac{1}{2}$ oz of sulphate of potash per sq yd. A fortnight later give $\frac{1}{2}$–$\frac{3}{4}$ oz of nitrate of soda per sq yd.

642 *Are leeks subject to disease or pests?*

The same as onions, but in practice trouble is uncommon.

643 *When will they be ready?*

From October on.

Lentils
644 *Are lentils easy to grow?*

Simply sow seed thinly outside in April in rows about 2 ft apart.

645 *What sort of soil do they need?*

Lentils will grow in most fairly dry soils.

646 *How do I know when the pods are ready?*

The leaves yellow and the pods darken. Of course it is the seeds themselves, not the pods which are used!

Lettuce
647 *What is cos lettuce?*

The kind with long, narrow leaves. Those sorts that make round heads are called cabbage lettuce.

648 *What are the main difficulties in growing lettuce?*

Lettuce will grow almost anywhere and in any soil, provided this can be kept moist and is reasonably rich, especially the top 8 in. Bolting is the main risk when the lettuce throws up a seeding head and leaves remaining are then useless.

649 *How can I prevent bolting?*

Some varieties are less likely to bolt than others, but in general you must keep the plants growing steadily. The nature of lettuce is to develop as long as good growing conditions allow and then, as soon as a check is felt, to throw out a flower and seed head. If you can keep them growing strongly they will not bolt.

650 *Does this call for a lot of soil preparation?*

Cultivation should be really thorough, with plenty of manure buried just below a spade depth. This will also act as a moisture reserve.

651 Should I give any other feeding?

Before planting, bonemeal, bone flour or superphosphate at about 3–4 oz per sq yd forked into the top few inches will help the plants to heart up quickly.

652 How can I produce a regular supply of lettuce throughout the year?

By making small sowings at frequent intervals rather than one or two large sowings. Plants grown in large groups will almost all come to maturity at the same time and will not keep.

653 What are the sowing times for lettuce outdoors?

In warm borders or under cloches you can sow as early as March, although it is better to wait until later in exposed places. Then continue seeding once a fortnight until August or even September.

654 Should lettuce be transplanted?

You can certainly use thinnings from the rows for planting out, but the best results appear to come from plants grown on in the position in which they are sown.

655 How much watering does lettuce require?

Deprived of nourishment or water, lettuce tends to bolt. Although they are fairly deep-rooted, regular watering is essential.

656 Do lettuce plants withstand the winter?

Yes, in most parts, provided a hardy variety is chosen and planted out 1 ft apart in autumn. If possible, shelter the bed from the north and east. Sow in late August and thin out to 9 in apart by October. In March, feed them with 2 oz of general fertiliser.

657 How can I get early lettuce?

Sow seed between January and March in a cool house or frame. Scatter seed broadcast and as they germinate pick the developing plants for salads, leaving the remainder to mature. Alternatively, grow seed in boxes and plant them out in April.

658 *Why is it that when I transplant, many of the plants fail?*

The lower leaves of the seedlings could be too low. Keep them clear of the soil to reduce risk of fungus attack.

659 *Why is it that when I sow lettuce, they seem to become overcrowded quickly and then, after thinning, those remaining look weak?*

You are sowing too thickly. Make drills $\frac{3}{4}$ in deep and 1 ft apart on a finely prepared seed bed. Sow very lightly, breaking up seed clusters with your fingers. Thin early, as soon as the first leaves appear, to 6 in apart.

660 *Isn't a 6 in spacing rather close?*

As they develop, alternate lettuce are picked out and eaten whilst small, so leaving the remainder 12 in apart to heart up and mature.

661 *Is winter lettuce hard to grow?*

Try sowing in frames in September and October and then pricking out the seedlings in a light but rich soil under glass, spaced about 3 in apart. As they grow, alternate plants can be pulled out and used, leaving the rest to grow on. Part of the crop can be put outside 6 in apart. Alternate ones again are removed for eating in the early part of winter. Give the remainder protection from the north.

662 *I find that lettuce in frames bolt more frequently. Can I prevent this?*

The frames must be airy and never allowed to dry out completely.

633 *How do you blanch cos lettuce?*

Simply tie the bunches of leaves together with raffia, just above the centre, shortly before cutting. This also helps hearting.

664 *What pests are a trouble with lettuce?*

Greenfly, which can be dealt with by dusting with Derris, and slugs, when the plants are young.

665 *How can I protect my young lettuce from slugs?*

Soot dusted around the seedlings helps and you can also buy proprietary slug killers.

666 *Some of my young lettuce seem to have been bitten off at the base. What causes this?*

It might be birds of course, but cutworms, grey caterpillar-like pests, can do this. Use Naphthalene hoed in near the plants.

Marjoram
667 *What is the difference between pot and sweet majoram?*

Sweet marjoram is generally preferred for flavouring purposes. It is perennial but is not perfectly hardy, so it is best to treat it like an annual. Pot marjoram has a slightly bitter taste and is a hardy perennial.

668 *Will the pot marjoram stand all year round outdoors?*

Yes, in the north though it is as well to give protection from cold winds in the winter. It must not be put in a damp position.

669 *How are the marjorams propagated?*

Sweet marjoram is grown from seed sown in warmth in March and put out 1 ft apart in May. Pot marjoram can be grown from seed in much the same way but it is usual to increase it by dividing mature roots, unless you want a large number of plants.

Marrow
670 *What varieties of marrow are there?*

The usual kinds are the 'courgette' bush type, grown where space is limited, and the trailing types, which cover several square yards of land. Their fruits taste much the same.

671 *To grow good marrows must I have plenty of rich manure?*

Marrows do like a rich soil, but provided your garden soil is in good heart and fertile, large amounts of farmyard manure are not needed.

672 *As I have some manure, what is the simplest way to use it?*

A straightforward method is to make small heaps of manure with about a barrow load of soil on top. The manure gives bottom heat and moisture and the marrows go ahead well in these conditions.

673 *How should I prepare an ideal bed outdoors?*

In the second week of May dig a 4 ft wide trench, 18 in deep and fill it with compost, leaves, old turves and partly rotted stable manure, heaping this up 9 in above soil level. Then replace the removed soil on top. On such a bed rich food is available for rapid growth. Some gardeners dig deeper, and finish the bed just below soil level, so making a slight hollow that retains water well in dry periods.

674 *Do marrows need any extra feeding?*

Marrows are gross feeders and like liquid manures especially, given weekly until about the middle of September. Do not give liquid manure until some of the marrows have set.

675 *What type of liquid manure should be used?*

1 oz each of superphosphate and sulphate of ammonia dissolved in a 2 gal can of water.

676 *How can I get early marrows?*

Sow under glass in February in pots or boxes. They will need heat at 18° C (65° F). Just press the seeds flat and firmly into the soil and the seedlings can be planted out as early as the beginning of May in a mild, sheltered area. Sow up to April in the same way.

677 *Can marrows be seeded outdoors?*

Yes; sow in May on the actual growing bed, putting 3 seeds
110

at each position 1½ in deep. Cover each seed with an upside down flower pot (with the hole blocked up). As the plants grow, remove the pots for lengthening periods during daylight. When the seedlings appear, choose the best and remove the other 2.

678 *When and how far apart are the plants spaced?*

Space in early June, the bush types 4 ft apart, and the trailers at double this spacing. (In any case these fruit better if you stop their trailers getting more than 4–5 ft long.)

679 *I only have a small family. How many marrow plants should I put in?*

1 trailing, or 3 bushy, should be enough unless you are very keen on them.

680 *Why are there 2 types of flower on my marrows?*

They are male and female. The one with the miniature marrow underneath is the female. For best results these must be fertilised.

681 *How is this done?*

Pull off one of the male flowers and take away its petals. Rub the centre of it into the centre of every female flower. Repeat this operation every few days.

682 *Why is it that some marrow plants that I have grown have not produced any female flowers at all?*

This does occasionally happen. Try pinching off the tips of the shoots. This sometimes starts the development of females.

683 *The marrows I grow are all very vigorous. Should I thin out the shoots?*

Pinch out any weak or infertile lengths at their bases.

684 *When will the first marrows be ready?*

From August on until the frosts.

685 *Should I cut the fruits as they reach the right size, or leave them on the plant until I am ready for them?*

111

To ensure the longest possible fruiting period always remove marrows as soon as they reach 2 lb weight, that is, about 9 in long. The skin should not be too tough to break with the thumb nail.

686 *How can I store them?*

Place them in boxes in single layers. The temperature must not drop below 13° C (55° F).

687 *What crops can be intercropped with vegetable marrow?*

You can put them out amongst spring cabbages, as soon as a few of these have been cut to make space. They will then grow on as the area is further cleared. Similarly, marrows can grow between early peas.

688 *What are the main problems of marrow growing?*

Fruit falling off at early stages of their development. This may be due to wet weather causing pollination to be ineffective. It is important to pollinate the plants several times. Moulds may be a trouble in damp seasons, while virus disease shows as yellow patching and mottling on the leaves. Slugs and greenfly also attack the leaves. Diseased plants are best burnt.

Melons
689 *Can I grow melons outdoors?*

Only in the warmest parts of the country. Make sure that you choose a variety not intended solely for the hothouse. They do prefer a frame, even a temporary one made of a few lengths of wood with glass over the top.

690 *How are they sown?*

It is often best to start the seed in pots with some warmth in spring, shifting them gradually to 5 in pots. When they are 1 ft high in early June they are ready for planting out, a yard apart.

691 *What sort of soil must I provide?*

Like marrows, they need a rich soil to provide for their rapid
112

growth. If you plant in frames, use a bucketful of John Innes No 3 compost.

692 *In general, what is their treatment?*

Treat like marrows and cucumbers. They have male and female flowers, identifiable because the female has a small fruit underneath it. These must be fertilised in the same way as marrows. It is best only to leave 6–8 fruits per plant to develop.

693 *Do the plants need containing like cucumbers?*

Yes; it is best to keep them fairly compact to increase the number of female flowers. Pinch out the main stem after 6 leaves have developed.

694 *When will the crop be ready?*

4-5 months after sowing.

695 *Is watering necessary?*

Yes, plenty, but stop all watering as fruit start ripening. This reduces splitting.

Mint
696 *Are there different kinds of mint?*

Yes, several, but the ordinary 'spear mint' is called Mentha viridis, whilst the 'apple mint', with a slightly sweeter flavour, is called Mentha rotundifolia.

697 *How can I prepare a mint bed?*

First of all obtain a few roots, keeping them covered with soft earth till you are ready to plant them. Dig the area deeply, incorporating rotted manure and a general fertiliser – leaf-mould is good if you have it, especially on light soil. Then plant the pieces in February, 9 in apart each way, about 2 in deep.

698 *How can I get mint in winter?*

In late autumn lift a few of the roots and put them in boxes. Bring these into a greenhouse or even on to a bright window sill in a moderately warm room. By having several boxes to bring in throughout the winter you can get a pretty regular supply.

699 *Mint seems to be very easy to grow; are there any problems?*

The main trouble is keeping it in bounds. The roots rapidly spread and you may end up with far more than you need! Many gardeners plant it initially in a bottomless old tin bath or bucket.

700 *What about diseases?*

The only one you might meet is a form of rust. To control this, dig up the whole plant, wash the roots completely clear of soil and heat them in water raised to 43° C (110° F) for about quarter of an hour. Then replant them in a different position.

701 *How can I maintain a good crop of young mint in dry summers?*

Keep well watered all the time.

702 *My mint is tending to get rather straggly and coarse and the leaves are losing something of their flavour. Can I improve the bed in any way?*

You can maintain a good crop of young mint in a dry summer by watering well. If flavour is impaired, remember that a mint bed benefits from renewal every 3–4 years, in autumn or spring.

703 *How is this renewal done?*

Dig up all the old plants, using a fork. Select young plants from the outside parts of each clump. You will not need very much, just 2–3 in of root and a few green buds on the top. Re-prepare the bed by deep digging and replant the young roots which soon spread.

704 *Should I re-make the mint bed in the same place?*

Unless you have been troubled by rust this is usually best. It is very difficult to get rid of mint roots entirely. If you use the old bed for some other plant you may find stalks of mint coming up for years.

Mushrooms

705 *Are mushrooms difficult to grow?*

Careful attention to detail is needed in preparing the beds. They are a little temperamental. Even if everything seems in order the crop may be poor. It is possible, however, to provide for a family's needs.

706 *Can't I encourage them to grow outside, without all the trouble of growing them indoors? After all, they do grow wild in fields.*

If you are fortunate enough to have a piece of grass where an occasional mushroom already appears, you can often increase the crop by planting spawn just below the grass. It is a hit-and-miss business though, compared to manure or compost-bed growing.

707 *What type of manure do I need and how is it prepared?*

The job is easiest with straw-based stable manue. Stack this at least 4 ft 6 in high. It will then heat up. Sprinkle water over any parts that dry out. 2 weeks later, turn the whole heap over and note the temperature with a large thermo-meter. It should now be about 65° C (150° F). A week later, turn it again. 4 days after that it should be warm and evenly brown. Aim at a temperature of about 27° C (80° F).

708 *Can I use a product other than stable manure?*

You can use ordinary straw which is made to rot down using compounds bought from mushroom spawn dealers. There are also special composts which only need wetting, though this method is more expensive.

709 *Where should the bed be made?*

Use any shed where an even temperature can be easily main-tained; the back of a warm garage perhaps, or a cellar.

710 *How is the manure arranged?*

115

Make it into a bed 1 ft high and 3 ft 6 in across. As soon as the temperature drops to 21° C (70° F) plant the spawn.

711 *What exactly is spawn?*

It is a seed. The mushrooms we eat are really the fruiting bodies of a fungus that grows mainly as a mass of white threads called mycelia. These threads become almost solid and can then be cut up into blocks. These blocks are sold commercially and are called spawn.

712 *How is spawn planted?*

Blocks of spawn are often marked with the planting size required. These pieces are about the size of an egg. Push them into holes 2 in deep and 9 in apart all ways. Squeeze the manure round the spawn, to crush out the air. Leave it for a fortnight after which the whole bed must be 'cased'.

713 *How is this done?*

Cover the heap completely with 2 in of moist, clean compost (preferably sterilised), patting it firmly into place, then add 1 ft of clean straw or hay all over.

714 *How can I grow mushrooms in boxes?*

Buy the special compost. Make this evenly damp and press it well down into deep boxes. Spawn, in smallish pieces, is pressed just below the surface and the whole box then stood in a warm place. This is often an effective and easy way of growing mushrooms on a small scale.

715 *What other work is needed before harvest?*

Just keep cold air from the heap.

716 *Is it necessary to grow mushrooms in the dark?*

No, but a dim light does seem to help.

717 *When I grew mushrooms on a flat bed method I found that mildew appeared all over the heap. Is this natural?*

No; you should take this off with a stiff broom.

Mustard and Cress

718 *Should I grow mustard and cress in boxes or on the open soil?*

It is easier to grow them (separately) in boxes, all year round. You can, however, successfully grow on open soil if you find this convenient.

719 *How is the seed sown?*

Use plenty. Outdoors, sprinkle over a fine soil surface, press gently and cover with dark polythene for 4 days until germination starts. Any container, even cardboard, can be used for seeding provided it has drain holes in the bottom. Put a handful of leaves for drainage in the bottom of each container and fill up with light soil, using a rammer to make it firm. Scatter seeds on the surface and pat them down gently. Cover with newspaper until germination.

720 *How warm must the temperature be indoors?*

About 13° C (55° F).

721 *I sowed mustard and cress but they were not ready at the same time. What did I do wrong?*

Sow the cress 3 days earlier than mustard and both will be ready together.

722 *Why does my cress crop often wilt away?*

This is 'damping off' caused by damp, stagnant air or poor soil. Try a sterilised compost and keep the plants airy.

Onions

723 *What type of soil is needed for onions?*

Onions need a fertile and well-drained soil and plenty of organic fertiliser, dug in below a spade depth. The ground must be firm and in full sun.

724 *Will onions grow in a new garden or heavy clay?*

Clay is not good for onions at the best of times and newly cultivated soil tends to encourage foliage growth rather than development of bulbs. It is better for onions to follow some other crop, perhaps cabbage or brussels sprouts, which will have been planted in deeply-dug ground.

725. My soil is on the light side; will this grow onions?

Try a dressing of Kainit, roughly 1 lb for every 15 sq yd, and ammonium sulphate at about half that rate.

726 Can I keep a bed specially for onions?

Onions do well in the same plot year after year.

727 Should I use any chemical fertilisers?

Apply either a mixture of 5 parts hoof and horn meal, 6 parts bonemeal and 2 parts sulphate of potash, or 2 parts super-phosphate and 1 part sulphate of potash instead.

728 What about lime?

Lime should not be overdone. The soil pH must never rise above 7.0.

729 Is soot beneficial?

It can be scattered over the final bed and dug in lightly.

730 Can I produce onions from seed?

As soon as the soil is fit to work (usually by March) sow outdoors, in rows a foot apart. Thin later to 6 in apart.

731 I have a greenhouse. Can I get earlier or better onions by seeding in heat?

Yes; sow in January, pricking out and gradually transferring them to small pots to put out finally in April.

732 How deep are onions sown?

On a very firm seed bed (roller or tread this down before-hand in dry weather), make drills $\frac{1}{4}$ in deep, 12 in apart. Do not sow thickly. (A scattering of powdered chalk up the drills will help you to see the black seeds.) Lightly tread them in.

733 How much seed will I need?

$\frac{1}{4}$ oz sows approximately 35 yd of row.

734 *Can some varieties be sown in autumn?*

Yes; put them in towards the end of August. Thin in spring to 6 in apart. (Use the thinnings for salads.) The remainder will be ready for lifting at the end of July. This kind often resist the onion fly well.

735 *I find it difficult to control weeds in the early stages of onion growth, or indeed to find the onions amid the growth of weeds! Can I prevent the weeds germinating?*

There are 'pre-emergence' weed killers which prevent the development of weeds for about 6 weeks. This gives a clear run for your developing onions. The makers' instructions must be carefully followed.

736 *What are onion 'sets'?*

These are very small, immature onions about $\frac{1}{2}$ in in diameter.

737 *What are the advantages of using onion sets instead of seeds?*

They require less work and are less susceptible to attack by the onion fly. They ripen earlier so are good for use in the north.

738 *How do I plant them?*

Make shallow drills, $\frac{1}{2}$ in deep and 1 ft apart. Place the bulbs root end downwards, 6 in apart. It is vital that they should be held firmly. Pat and tread the soil around and between them to hold them down with their tops just visible.

739 *How much watering do onions need?*

In a dry summer plenty of water is especially important.

740 *What about fertiliser?*

Give a mixed fertiliser or liquid manure every fortnight.

741 *Why do some of my onions break off at ground level?*
Probably they were too shallowly planted. However, too deep planting may lead to a thickening of their necks.

742 *My onions fail to ripen up in wet summers.*

Try covering with cloches but leave 3 in spaces between the cloches and bend over the onion tops.

743 *Some of my onions are throwing up small flower stems from the middle. Should I leave these on?*

No; take them off as soon as they appear.

744 *How do I know when onions are ripe?*

The foliage starts to yellow. Bend the neck of the leaves at right angles, toward the north, to speed up ripening. Also slide a fork underneath each bulb and lever it upwards slightly. 2 weeks later the plants can be finally lifted and dried.

745 *How can I get really large onions?*

Deep trenching is required, and heavy manuring, as early as possible in winter. Then sow plants in boxes in gentle heat, using a John Innes compost. Harden these off in cold frames and plant out in April. Provide wide spacing, about 18 in, and liquid feeds every week.

746 *What causes light, blueish patches on leaves, some of which have shrivelled up?*

Mildew like this is common in wet seasons on badly drained soil. Try spraying with copper fungicide or Bordeaux mixture in spring. It is probably best to burn the crop and keep the land free of onions for 2–3 years.

747 *What is white rot?*

This causes the foliage to turn yellow and at the base of the bulb you will find a fluffy fungus growth, perhaps with black spots.

748 *What should I do with diseased plants?*

Unless the plants are immediately burnt they will contaminate the soil. Onions cannot then be grown on the land for 8–10 years.

749 *Isn't there any way of curing or preventing it?*

Calomel dust controls less serious infestations. Pour 1 lb for every 20 yd of row, into the open drills just before sowing. Repeat if wet weather follows.

750 Are there any other diseases of onions?

Onion smut is one, largely prevented by watering seed drills with 1 gall of 2% solution of formalin for every 50 yd run.

751 How can the onion fly be detected?

The signs are yellow, wilted leaves. Calomel dust used against white rot kills onion fly eggs and maggots too.

752 Are spring onions for salads easy to grow?

Yes. Sow in late summer and early autumn in well-drained beds. Make several other sowings between March and May.

753 How do I sow them?

Fairly thickly; the pullings you make to thin them out can be eaten, the remainder will gradually fill the rows.

754 What about onions for pickling?

Seed for this purpose is sown in March, rather thickly and scattered, not in drills. These will be ready in June or July.

755 Does this type require any special seed bed?

The bed must be completely free of weeds and very finely raked. Curiously enough, pickling onions appear to do better on rather poor, dry soil.

756 Are onions best stored in strings hanging up?

Yes, or try hanging a horizontal net of wire netting near the roof of your shed and spreading the onions evenly over this.

757 What are potato onions?

These are a variety that produce small onion bulbs underground. They are grown like shallots.

758 And tree onions?

These are the opposite to potato onions. They produce

groups of small onions at the tops of stems. Again they are treated like shallots, the bulbs being planted in spring. Later, you can increase them by planting the young bulbs or dividing the base bulb.

759 *I'm told there is also a Welsh onion.*

Yes; this is a perennial plant, the leaves and stems only being used for flavouring, not as a main vegetable. It is increased by division in early spring, or by seed sown in April.

Parsley
760 *I sowed parsley seed but it seemed to come up very sparsely and slowly so I dug it in again. What did I do wrong?*

Parsley takes a long time to germinate. Next time, soak the seed in warm water and make sure the soil is moist before sowing. Seeding times are March, May and August.

761 *What is the right sowing depth?*

Sow 1 in deep, in drills 1 ft apart. Thin later to 9 in apart.

762 *Should I let the plants flower?*

No; remove the buds.

763 *How do I get winter parsley?*

Put a cloche over the plants in late autumn and they will keep growing for quite a time. Alternatively, pot them and stand them on a bright windowsill or in a greenhouse.

764 *I would like to try this but few of my plants have leaves by that time.*

Cut the plants well back in August. This will cause them to bush out with more leaves which will see you through the autumn and early winter.

Parsnips
765 *What ground is best for parsnips?*

They prefer fertile but rather light soil. However, any deep, well-worked soil will give a fair crop.

766 *Do parsnips need extra manuring?*

In general no, especially if they follow a crop which has had deep digging and manuring. 4 oz of a general fertiliser can be added before sowing.

767 *Is it best to sow in drills or singly?*

To get the best parsnips the single seed method is better. Make deep holes with a dibber or iron bar, a foot apart, and fill these up with fine soil. In February or March put in a couple of seeds 1 in deep on the top of each hole. Remove the weakest of the two plants as they germinate. This will give excellent, straight parsnips.

768 *This seems a lot of work. Drilling is presumably less trouble?*

Yes, though with drilling you have to thin out to 9 in apart. Never transplant the thinnings however.

769 *When are parsnips sown?*

Usually in March or April, in drills 1 in deep and 18 in apart. Thin them first to 3 in apart, and then gradually take out more to leave the best 9 in apart.

770 *When are parsnips lifted?*

They taste better if you let the frost get at them slightly, so wait until October.

771 *Do parsnips have diseases?*

The carrot fly can be harmful and can open the way for canker attack. Prevention is better than cure. Dust naphthalene or gamma BHC over the soil near the plants.

Peas

772 *There seem to be three general kinds, 'earlies', 'second earlies' and 'late'. When are they sown?*

Earlies in February and March; Second Earlies in April; Late in May and Earlies again in June.

773 *What is the difference between round-seeded and wrinkled-seeded varieties?*

Round-seeded sorts are hardy, good for risky sowings early in spring. Wrinkled-seeded are sweeter.

774 *How long after sowing will the peas be ready?*

11–12 weeks for early varieties; 12–13 for second earlies; late take 14–15 weeks. However June early peas may be ready in only 8 weeks.

775 *Can I grow early peas without glass?*

When attempting to grow early vegetables of any kind a south- or south-west-facing slope is always best. Early pea sowings must be done as soon as the soil has become drained of excess winter moisture. February is a possible month in the warmer parts of the country. In northern areas however you may have to wait until April.

776 *I am told some gardeners sow peas in September; is this safe?*

Hardy varieties sown in September and crowned with cloches will see winter through and give very early crops.

777 *What basic cultivation do peas need?*

Peas must root deeply for success, so a really deep cultivation is essential. If the soil tends to be overdrained, spongy material such as a peat or farmyard manure should be dug in as deeply as possible. This acts as a moisture reservoir.

778 *What other fertilisers are needed?*

It helps to give superphosphate at 2–3 oz per sq yd on most soils, and you can also add $\frac{1}{2}$–1 oz of sulphate of potash. Scattering weathered wood ash along the seed drills is commonly done. Do not give nitrogen.

779 *How are the peas sown, and at what spacing?*

Take out a flat, 9 in wide drill about 3 in deep and scatter or arrange the seeds so that they average 3 in apart. Alternatively sow in straight drills 2 in deep. The soil must be fairly dry.

780 *Is there any way I can speed up the drying of the soil?*

A week before sowing fork over the whole bed 8 in deep, leaving the soil as open as possible. Repeat this forking every 2 days, finally sowing on a dry day. Rake the soil flat in the morning and sow in late afternoon.

781 *How far apart should pea rows be?*

Usually the same distance is allowed between rows as the eventual height of the mature plant, as shown on the packet.

782 *Isn't this wasteful of space?*

Plant quick-growing crops between the rows, such as lettuce, spinach or turnips.

783 *How many peas must I buy?*

Like beans, peas are brought traditionally by the pint. 1 pint sows about 25 yd of drill.

784 *How can I prevent pea seeds from being eaten by birds, rats and mice?*

Moisten the seeds and sprinkle red lead powder over them, shaking them up well in a bottle. This protects the seeds themselves from mice and birds. You can protect the germinating plants from birds with small-mesh wire netting in thin strips, half rolled archway-like along the row. Place supporting stakes on either side of the netting for the peas to cling to as they grow through it.

785 *What is the main problem in starting early peas?*

Avoiding damp conditions, which favour fungus attack and may prevent the seed from germinating properly.

786 *I never seem to get a good row of pea seedlings. How can I prevent some plants failing?*

You cannot always prevent it. Sow a dozen extra peas to fill gaps as they appear.

787 *In our area it is difficult to obtain natural pea sticks. What else can I use?*

Dwarf peas can often stand without supports. It is also

possible to grow peas directly up wire or plastic netting stretched between frames of wood.

788 *Should pea sticks tilt inwards or be upright?*

Bushy pea sticks are best and should be stuck in upright on either side of a row.

789 *After germination, what cultivation do young peas need?*

Thin out crowded plants and slightly earth up the remainder. All peas need moist conditions so it is vital to prevent the surface caking into a dry, hard pan in hot weather. Keep the hoe moving to reduce soil evaporation and water as frequently as possible.

790 *How can I obtain the largest possible pea pods?*

Space the plants further apart than usual. Stop them growing 18 in short of their normal height. Feed regularly with liquid manure (with little nitrogen). Of course exhibition-size peas must be grown in deeply trenched, well-manured soil. The pods must be thinned out by hand to avoid crowding. (Closely spaced pods give heavy crops but the individual pods are smaller than those which are wider spaced.)

791 *Can I prevent many of my pea pods being only half filled?*

Once the first flowers drop, scatter 1 oz of superphosphate per yd along the rows and water it in. Empty pods can also be due to drought, lack of pollinating insects or too rich soil, especially excess nitrogen.

792 *What is the real value of putting grass mowings along the rows of peas?*

It tends to prevent the peas dying back early in summer. It keeps the ground cool and moist underneath. You can also use straw litter or an inch or so of compost.

793 *How can I prevent pea pods in late summer which develop high on the bushes not filling up properly? I have tried fertilising them without much success.*

Thin out the bottom of the plants, removing weak shoots

which are not carrying many pods, and cut off the stems above the pods on the remaining shoots. Clear fully harvested plants away immediately or they may be attacked by mildew which may spread to the remaining plants. Do not however dig out the roots.

794 Why shouldn't I dig out pea roots?

Peas and beans have the power to fix nitrogen from the air, providing valuable fertiliser. They store this in their roots, which left in place and later dug in enrich the soil. Alternatively, lift and place them on the compost heap. Never burn them.

795 Can I grow peas in winter?

Only in a greenhouse kept at at least 10°C (50°F) at night and about 18°C (65°F) during the day. Dwarf plants can be sown in compost from mid-November to March in succession and should be ready for picking about the middle of March.

796 What type of compost is best?

Use 2 parts fertile loam, 1 part leaf-mould or peat, $\frac{1}{4}$ part of coarse sand and add $1\frac{1}{2}$oz of superphosphate and $\frac{1}{2}$ oz of potash sulphate to each 2 buckets full of compost.

797 Can I raise peas in cold frames for early planting out?

This is a fine method for getting the earliest possible crops. Sow 9–10 seed to each 5 in pot in early December. Thin the plants after germination to 5–6 per pot. They do not require much heat, but must be well lit and given plenty of fresh air whenever the weather allows. Planting out is done after the middle of March, preferably on a south-west-facing border.

798 How can I avoid disturbing peas which have been grown on early in boxes when I transplant them?

Sow the peas in specially made narrow boxes, from which the bottoms can be removed. They can then be stood in a planting trench and easily slid out, complete with soil.

799 *How can I tell when peas and beans are ready to harvest?*

Only by opening the pods. They are better picked younger than older!

800 *Is it true that there are peas that you can eat without shelling?*

The sugar pea is grown in exactly the same way as ordinary green peas and can be cooked without shelling. The pods do not have a tough, stringy, inner layer to their edges.

801 *What about diseases?*

On maturing plants, virus disease is shown by irregular discoloration and yellow mottling of the leaves. Plants attacked should be burnt. Occasionally you will see mildew on late peas. This can be cured by spraying with a copper-based fungicide, and giving plenty of water.

802 *What causes the dark red spots on many of my peas?*

This is probably caused by a deficiency of manganese in the soil and it is not a disease in the ordinary sense. You can cure this in future by watering the plants as they come into bloom with a solution of manganese sulphate, dissolving $1\frac{1}{2}$ oz in 20 gal of water.

803 *What are the small grubs I find inside many of my peas?*

These are probably grubs of the pea moth. Prevention is the only cure here. As the flowers open, treat them with Derris or spray containing dimethoate or menazon. These kill the female moth before it lays any eggs.

804 *The edges of my pea plants seem to have been chewed by an insect, taking out small, half-round bites. What is causing this?*

This is probably the pea and bean weevil. Protect the plants with an insecticide spray as soon as the first traces appear.

Potatoes
805 *Why is the potato so often recommended as a first crop for a first new vegetable garden?*

The potato has no particular virtue in itself on new land, nor does it help to clear weeds (as is sometimes stated). It is the work which is done on the soil in growing potatoes that improves the land. Deep digging, manuring and planting of the seed tubers is followed by earthing at intervals. Weed growth and regrowth is therefore kept down for much of the season. If the ground is then turned over again after the potatoes have been lifted, weeds will once again be discouraged.

806 *What factors might prevent having a good potato crop?*

Infertile soil and badly drained conditions do not suit potatoes. They tolerate light or heavy soils but damp is dangerous. Make sure that the potato patch is drained well. Deep digging which incorporates rich natural organic fertilisers such as farmyard manure gives ideal conditions. This also makes the subsequent 'earthing up' much easier.

807 *What is 'earthing up'?*

As potato stems (haulms) grow, the soil between the rows is drawn up in ridges to half-bury them. This is done first when the haulms are about 8 in high and again a week or two later when they have grown further. Earthing helps against disease, the potatoes develop better and are easier to lift.

808 *A friend grows early crops without earthing up at all.*

If the spacing between the rows is reduced by 6 in or so this will often be adequate for the early crops. Remember though that the work of earthing up itself improves the quality of the garden soil.

809 *What other fertilisers are needed?*

Add 4 oz per sq yd of a general purpose fertiliser. 4 parts superphosphate, 3 of sulphate of ammonia and 2 of sulphate of potash will serve. This is not however a full substitute for farmyard manure, which improves the texture of the soil as well as its chemical contents.

810 *Should I apply lime?*

9

It is not normally necessary, unless the land is already very acid.

811 *How are potatoes planted?*

Buy seed tubers certified free of virus, and in winter stand them 'eyes' up in boxes in a light but frost-proof place at least 5°C (40°F). Sprouts will spring from the 'eyes'. Keep the strongest 2–3 sprouts and rub the others off.

812 *Can't tubers be planted straight away?*

You get a crop several weeks earlier than if unsprouted tubers are planted.

813 *Can I grow really early potatoes?*

This depends largely on where you live. The earlier the seed tubers are in the ground, perhaps in February in a south- or west-facing bed, the sooner they will be ready to lift. In the colder parts of the country though, it is not safe to plant before April, and the harvest will be that much later.

814 *Do such early potatoes need special fertilising?*

Try a mix of 8 parts of superphosphate, 5 of sulphate of ammonia and 3 of sulphate of potash at 4 oz per sq yd. This is rather richer than main crop fertiliser.

815 *Can early potatoes be forced?*

'Sprout' the seed tubers and plant them in January 2 in below the surface in boxes or pots or soil kept in a warm greenhouse or frame. Tubers will form in the soil and by April the entire plants can be tipped gently out, the tubers picked away and then the plant replaced for further growth. These 'miniature' potatoes often have the finest flavour, though perhaps it is just their newness which gives them their special appeal!

816 *How big should seed potatoes be?*

The size of an egg.

817 *How are they planted?*

Draw the dug soil into ridges. Place the tubers along the

hollows between the ridges. Then pull the ridge soil over the tubers so that they are under the ridges, buried about 6 in deep. In weedy soil, plant on the flat, but draw soil up round the shoots as these push upwards. This 'works' the soil and keeps weeds down.

818 *How wide apart are potatoes planted?*

Plant earlies with 24 in between rows, and the tubers 15 in apart; second earlies, 27 in between rows, tubers 18 in apart; main-crop 30 in between rows with tubers 18 in apart.

819 *What weight of seed should I buy?*

Use 7 lb for each 30 yd row.

820 *Should I save some tubers from each crop as seed for the following year?*

It is better to buy new seed every year. There is usually a slight deterioration in the quality of the plants if you save your own tubers for seed. You can do it for 1–2 years by choosing rather small tubers from the healthiest plants. The cost of the seed tubers is, however, so small in relation to the value of the crop that this is hardly worth the risk.

821 *Can potatoes be grown under black polythene sheet 'weed-suppressors'?*

Cut cheap black polythene into long strips about a yard wide. Dress the soil with a good mixed fertiliser, lay the strips along the rows and slash the polythene crosswise every foot. Plant early variety tubers in mid-March below the holes. They will soon grow through. Earthing up will not be possible.

822 *When are potatoes ready to lift?*

First Earlies in June; Second Earlies in July; Main-Crop from August.

823 *How do I know when they are ready?*

Flowers appear on earlies. With the others, broadly speaking, the leaves turn yellow. It is fairly easy to distinguish the even-coloured natural yellowing as leaves mature from the patchy mottling accompanying virus disease, which in any case usually occurs earlier in the season.

824 *Is this the same as blight?*

No; blight is a fungus disease, one of the worst that can attack potatoes in this country. Although the disease is often present, it is commoner in wet seasons than dry.

825 *Is there a cure?*

It is better to prevent the disease than try to cure it. Cut off and burn all infected foliage.

826 *How do I prevent blight?*

Spraying with Bordeaux mixture or other fungicide sprays based on copper is the usual method. Do this in the South about the end of June or beginning of July, in the Midlands in July and in the North and Scotland at the end of July or the first week in August, depending on the weather. The spray must reach under the leaves as well as on top. Repeat the spray after a 3 week interval.

827 *What other diseases are common on potatoes?*

Common scab shows itself as rough raised spots on the skin of the potatoes. These are removed in peeling. It is, strictly speaking, not a serious disease but it is very unpleasant to see. If you use new seed stock and earth up properly on fertile soil you will probably not get this trouble.

828 *Is black scab different?*

This is another similar disease which can be prevented by selecting varieties immune to it.

829 *What disease causes potato leaves to become discoloured, mottled and twisted?*

These are virus infections. The leaves may eventually turn brown and wither and are sometimes dwarfed, with crushed stems packed closely together.

830 *Are potatoes edible from such virus-infected plants?*

They are safe to eat but should never be used for seed or the infection will be carried on.

831 *Is there no treatment?*

None that is effective.

832 *What pests are a trouble when growing potatoes?*

The worst of all is the colorado beetle, which you are legally bound to report to the Ministry of Agriculture.

833 *How can I recognise it?*

The beetle itself is a very distinctive oval yellow shape with striking black lengthways stripes. You may see orange eggs laid in masses on the leaves or red grubs with black spots that eat the potato leaves.

834 *What less important pests are there?*

Eelworm attack is quite serious. These leave small, white lumps on the tubers and roots. There is no good remedy except letting the land remain free of potatoes for several years. Other pests are wireworms and leatherjackets which damage the tubers by direct attack, and caterpillars of some moths also eat the leaves. Insecticides will usually deal with these.

835 *How can I keep slugs out of my early potatoes?*

Take out the planting drills early, and scatter along them a 50–50 mixture of powdered copper sulphate and ground limestone, at a rate of 1lb to every 50 yd. Plant a month later.

836 *How do I prepare potatoes for storage?*

The first essential is to allow them to dry naturally as soon as you dig them out. Leave them on the soil surface till their skins are hardened. This takes about half a day. Then heap up the dried potatoes on straw and cover them with another straw layer followed by a layer of soil. This 'clamp' should be on a well-drained site, preferably a little above the surrounding soil level.

837 *Do I put both the straw and soil coverings on at once?*

No, apply the straw first and leave for 2 weeks before covering the whole lot with about 10 in of soil. To ensure ventilation leave a 'chimney' in the top of the heap consisting of a vertical bunch of straw. This allows air to pass up from the heap freely.

838 *This all seems a lot of trouble. Can I store them in any simpler way?*

You can keep them in boxes in a dark, dry place. Never expose them to the light or they will turn green, which makes them poisonous. Powdered sulphur sprinkled over stored potatoes helps them to resist mildew.

Pumpkin
839 *My children would like to grow a pumpkin. What treatment will it need?*

The pumpkin needs practically the same treatment as the marrow. You do though need lots of space.

840 *What differences are there from the marrow?*

Water and feed until the fruit is full sized, then reduce water but leave them in place until September. The fewer fruits you have to grow (5 maximum) the bigger they will be.

Radish
841 *I suppose radishes are very easy to grow in any conditions?*

In spite of their popularity and small size radishes are not easy to grow to perfection, though with a little trouble you can get supplies nearly all the year round.

842 *What are the main needs for growing good radish?*

Besides fertile soil, which all rapidly growing plants need, steadily moist soil conditions are vital. Thin out early so that none of the developing seedlings actually touch each other.

843 *What type of fertiliser should I give them?*

Compost and leaf-mould are useful in most soils, especially

134

the lighter kinds. As a boost to this, give 4 oz of a general fertiliser per sq yd, raked lightly into the top few inches of soil.

844 *How can I get crops all year round?*

You must have a frame for sowing from December to February. The first outdoor sowings are made in early March in a sheltered spot. Sow only a little at a time at 2–3 week intervals until September to give you a succession of crops. Crops to eat in winter are helped by a light top dressing of sulphate of ammonia in September which makes sure that the plants are pushed well ahead before the cold weather.

845 *How deeply are they seeded?*

Sow 1 in deep and in rows 4–5 in apart.

846 *Do they need thinning out?*

Careful fine seeding is essential, followed by early thinning to space the plants so that the mature radishes will just touch.

847 *How much seed should be used?*

1 oz of seed sows 30 yd of row.

848 *Can't I leave the radish out in the winter?*

Winter radish varieties are sown in July in rows a foot apart. Thin later. In mild areas maturing radish can be left out until required, perhaps protected by litter scattered over the surface. In harder districts it may be better to lift them before the frosts and store them, packed in sand, in cool, dark conditions.

849 *How can I prevent radish becoming strong and stringy?*

This is almost always caused by lack of water. It is vital to water the ground thoroughly a week before sowing and to ensure that the ground never completely dries out during the growing period. Radish need a rapid and unchecked growth. Good summer radishes, in July or August, are hard to grow.

850 *Presumably such small plants can be used for inter-cropping between others?*

Yes, radish mature so rapidly that you can grow them between pea or bean rows or celery trenches, or even in the same drills as lettuce, onions and carrots. In this last case the seed itself is mixed. The radishes push ahead and are pulled out before the others have really started.

851 *Are radishes subject to disease?*

They are 'brassicas' and diseases such as club root affect them, while the turnip gall weevil and flea beetle can also be troublesome at times. The same treatments as for the larger plants will serve if necessary. Birds like radish, so protection by strings or netting is also needed.

Rampion
852 *Can you suggest any other unusual plant for winter salads?*

The white roots of rampion can be peeled and chopped for salads throughout the winter. Sow several drills at intervals between March and April, about a foot apart.

853 *Has rampion any special needs?*

It is a good crop for an exceptionally shady position, provided you can keep it well fed. It does not do well on poor soil.

854 *When is it ready for picking?*

Through autumn and winter, though it is best to lift all the roots in November and store them, packed in sand, in a dry place.

Rhubarb
855 *Can I grow rhubarb plants from seed?*

It is possible, but it takes 3 years for seedlings to reach pulling size, so it is more usual to buy plants.

856 *How are new plants put in?*

Plant 2 in deep and a yard apart, in spring. Do not plant in winter, or when heavy rain is expected.

857 *Isn't there a rapidly maturing type for growing from seed?*

The 'Gaskins Perpetual' variety is a quick developer.

858 *When is rhubarb seed sown?*

Most varieties very early in the year in a warm greenhouse or frame. Outdoors not before March or April. Make drills a foot apart, thin seedlings to 6 in apart and transplant them to a final spacing of about 3 ft in autumn or the following spring. 'Gaskins Perpetual' can be sown under glass in March for planting out by May.

859 *What is the usual way of preparing a rhubarb bed?*

Rhubarb is an exceptionally gross feeder. Since it remains in the same place year after year it pays to give the ground deep cultivation, digging in as much organic manure as possible.

860 *Do I need stable manure, or will chemicals do?*

Stable and farmyard manure have many advantages, providing fertilising chemicals, improving the texture of most soils and acting as a moisture reserve. Rhubarb must never dry out or it does not crop well.

861 *What type of chemicals might be used to help out a shortage of rich farm manures?*

All the bone products, bone flour and hoof and horn meal, are beneficial. Dressings of nitrogen stimulate growth, especially during and immediately after the pulling period. Sulphate of ammonia is suitable, but any rich, liquid manure serves very well. It is very hard to over-feed rhubarb.

862 *Does rhubarb grow in shade?*

It can actually grow almost anywhere, but does best in a sunny but not dry position.

863 *How much watering is needed?*

In dry seasons watering rhubarb will rapidly speed the growth. Remember, most of the stems are in fact water and without constant supplies they cannot develop satisfactorily.

864 *When can I start pulling from a newly planted bed?*

You might be able to pull one or two sticks the year after planting, but don't take any later than June. Main cropping starts the year after.

865 *On an established bed, can I pull all season through?*

Commercial growers often stop pulling about the end of June to allow the plants to re-establish themselves during the later part of the summer. You can carry on a month later in small gardens, provided you always leave a few large leaves to each crown.

866 *Are rhubarb leaves edible?*

No; they are very poisonous.

867 *My rhubarb has thrown up large flower plants. Are these harmful?*

Rhubarb must never flower as it weakens the plant for a season or more.

868 *How can I improve a very old bed of rhubarb?*

If the bed is doing well then there is no need to interfere with it, but if the stems are becoming sparse, weak and thin it is then best to lift the whole bed, deeply dig the ground and divide the plants. Each division should have one or more crowns which are replanted like new plants.

869 *Should this be done at any particular interval?*

Every 4–5 years.

870 *How can I force rhubarb for early supplies?*

In January or February cover crowns (not less than 2 years old) with open-ended buckets, barrels, tubs or boxes. Many gardeners also surround the outside of these with stable or farmyard manure. This gives warmth but is not essential, especially on good soil in warm areas.

871 *Can I force plants earlier still bringing them indoors?*

Dig up a selection of the plants in November. Leave them outdoors to be 'frosted' for about 3 weeks. Then bring them into a warm shed or greenhouse, up to 24°C (75°F), and plant the roots in boxes of soil kept in deep shade. It is essential to spray frequently with tepid water to keep the soil moist and the stems will develop in 4–5 weeks.

872 *Should I cut or pull rhubarb?*

Always pull rhubarb and make sure that you get the very base of the stem. Short pieces of broken stem left attached can cause rot.

Sage
873 *When are sage cuttings put in?*

Plant in April or September. When taking the cuttings, pull small stems off with a 'heel' of the main stem bark sticking to the bottom ends. This type of heeled cutting roots quicker than a straight cutting.

874 *Where should I plant sage?*

In the sun, in a well-drained spot.

875 *My sage plants appear to have been frosted. What should I do?*

Cut the whole plant down to 8 in tall. New shoots will grow.

876 *How do I dry sage?*

It can be force dried in an oven at about 37°C (100°F), laid out on papers or metal sheets. Keep it in glass jars. Parsley, thyme and marjoram can be dealt with in the same way, perhaps at a little higher temperature, say 50°C (112°F). Sage is frequently used in stuffings for poultry or with cheese and salads.

Salsify
877 *What is salsify?*

It is a root crop, rather like parsnips but with a better flavour. It is also known as the vegetable oyster.

878 *I always thought chards were a form of salsify?*

The word chard is sometimes used for blanched, flowering shoots of salsify which have been left over the winter and push up in spring. Chard is a word also used to describe the shoots of globe artichoke.

879 *What type of soil does salsify need?*

Anywhere exposed to full sun. It does not do well in shade. It needs rich ground that has been deeply dug and manured earlier with plenty of old farm manure well worked in. 2 oz per yd of general fertiliser before seeding helps too.

880 *How is it grown from seed?*

Sow in April, $\frac{1}{2}$ in deep and in rows 15 in apart. It can be thinned out later to 9 in between plants. They are ready in late October. For winter use, sow in May.

881 *Are the plants lifted then or can they be left out?*

Either, though it is best not to leave them too long in very cold areas. Store them packed in peat or dry sand.

Savory
882 *What is the difference between the summer and winter savory herbs?*

Summer savory is an annual that likes the sun and can be sown in April and thinned to a foot apart all ways. Winter savory is a perennial which might be raised from seed but is usually propagated by division early in spring. For year-round supplies, plant both.

883 *How is summer savory harvested?*

As the flower stems appear, cut them off entire and tie in bunches to hang in a cool place. Summer savory is best for culinary use and has a piquant, slightly peppery taste.

884 *Does the perennial winter savory need any special attention?*

Simply cut back all the old shoots in spring. This will force new growth.

Savoy

885 *Does savoy cabbage require special treatment?*

The main advantage of the savoy is its extreme hardiness so it is best for use in the North. It is treated much the same as cabbage.

886 *When are sowings made?*

For late autumn sow in March. For winter crops, mid April to the end of May will do.

887 *What spacing is needed?*

18 in apart all ways or perhaps a little more.

888 *Do they need fertilisers?*

Like all leafy crops, nitrogen is needed. Give this in a handful of sulphate of ammonia per yard near planting time, but do not give nitrogen after midsummer or the plants will not harden up for the winter.

Scorzonera

889 *I have heard of a vegetable called scorzonera. What is it like and how is it treated?*

Scorzonera is a crop with long, blackish-purple roots of tender flavour. It is rather like salsify.

890 *How is it grown?*

Like carrots or parsnips, sow outdoors in May. It needs deep soil that has not been freshly fed with manures. Sow seed 1 in deep in rows a foot apart and thin the seedlings down to 6 in apart later. They are ready in autumn.

891 *What advantage has scorzonera over salisfy?*

Scorzonera is hardy and can be left in the ground during winter.

Seakale

892 *Are the roots of this tasty winter vegetable easy to grow?*

Yes, and you can keep a bed going for years after starting off with only a few roots, bought from nurserymen.

893 *It isn't grown from seed then?*

It can be, but it takes 3 years from seed sown in March or April to reach edible size.

894 *What soil is needed for seakale roots?*

Any fairly deep soil, well limed, will serve.

895 *How are the roots planted?*

Many nurserymen call young roots 'thongs'. Plant them with their top ends (usually cut off square, not slanting) an inch below the surface, in March, 2 ft apart. As they sprout, retain only the strongest shoot.

896 *What is the next step?*

In November, lift all the plants and take off side-roots 6 in long to give next season's supply of thongs. (Cut the bottom ends slanting, as they must be planted right way up.) Store these thongs in bundles, sunk in dry sand.

897 *What happens to the main roots, once the thongs are taken?*

Store them outdoors under sand and at intervals bring one or two into warmth. Sink them in boxes of soil moistened with warm water, in total darkness. Forced new shoots will be ready for cutting (at 6 in long) in about 5 weeks.

898 *Can seakale be forced without lifting them?*

Simply cover the plants with pots or boxes in January.

899 *Should seakale be allowed to flower?*

No. Pinch out all flower stems.

900 *Is it true that seakale benefits from salt?*

You can scatter a handful of salt around each seakale plant during June and July.

901 *My seakale appear to have a fungus attack. What should I treat it with?*

Do not try. It is better to dig up and burn (not compost) any attacked plant. Extra lime next season may help.

Seakale Beet
902 *What is seakale beet?*

This is a useful and easily produced vegetable grown for its thick stalks and leaves. These are both cooked, the stalks like seakale, the leaves like spinach.

903 *When is it sown?*

Early in April. After germination thin plants to about a foot apart. You should get a crop by autumn carrying on until mid-winter.

904 *Does seakale beet need special fertiliser?*

It likes rich soil for best results and any sort of stable manure or compost does well. Give it also a general fertiliser in summer to keep it growing vigorously.

Shallots
905 *Are shallots easy to grow?*

Yes, probably the easiest of all the onion family. They are useful where ordinary onions suffer from onion fly.

906 *Are they grown from seed or bulbs?*

Seed can be sown in March in drills 9 in apart, but the seedlings mature rather slowly so it is customary to plant bulbs instead.

907 *How should I put them in?*

In February or March press into the surface 9 in apart, 1 ft between rows.

908 *Are the bulbs completely covered on planting?*

On no account; the point of the bulb must show through the soil after planting.

909 *Does the ground need any fertilisers?*

If the soil has previously been well dug and manured for

some earlier crop it does not need much additional fertiliser. A fairly generous dressing of superphosphate, about 4–5 oz per sq yd, can be forked into the topsoil just before planting. Make sure the ground is reasonably firm.

910 *Can they be combined with other crops?*

Try planting them on the soil ridges beside your celery crop. They can be harvested before the celery earthing starts.

911 *Do they need any special attention during the year?*

Shallots grow quite rapidly, producing a cluster of bulblets in July when they are coming up to maturity. You can then draw the soil away from them to allow them to ripen.

912 *What is the most compact way of dealing with shallots in a small area?*

You can grow shallots in a $3\frac{1}{2}$ in pot sunk into the soil up to the rim.

913 *Are the flower heads of shallots left on?*

No; pick them off as they appear.

914 *When lifting shallots should the leaves be cut off or left on?*

Leave them on, allowing them to dry out naturally.

915 *Am I planting shallots too shallowly, as I find they tend to lift out of the ground soon after planting?*

At all events the shallots must never have their noses buried. Try pushing them more firmly down and squeezing the soil around and beside them. Too firm ground below the top inch may be the trouble. The roots cannot force through, so lift the bulbs instead as they lengthen.

916 *When are shallots finally lifted?*

Lift at the end of July or early August, as the stems start to die off. Remove loose skins before storing. They will keep till March or later in a dry place. Check occasionally for soft rot, a disease affecting under-ripe bulbs.

917 *What are the worst pests of shallots?*

The usual onion pests, some of which can be discouraged by scattering ashes over the newly planted bulbs. Birds must also be kept off by netting.

Spinach

918 *Are spinach and perpetual spinach varieties of the same plant?*

They are different plants but have the same food purpose. The perpetual spinach is a variety of beet and produces large leaves. Spinach itself is easily grown as an annual, seeded crop.

919 *Is it true that there are 2 types of ordinary spinach too?*

Yes, the round-seeded summer spinach, which is not hardy, and the hardy winter spinach, which has prickly seeds. Keep both sorts very well watered. They do not like hot and dry conditions.

920 *How do I grow summer spinach?*

Sow small quantities of seed at intervals from early March through into July or even later, 1 in deep, with the rows a foot apart. Thin the plants down to 9 in apart after germination.

921 *How much seed will I need?*

1 oz of seed sows 50 yd, and is usually enough for a whole season's supply. Do not put it all in at once. Instead, sow 5 separate rows, each 10 yd long, at fortnightly intervals. Soak the seed for a day beforehand.

922 *How can I get spinach in winter?*

The prickly seeded winter spinach can be sown from July to September, spaced out later to 3–4 in apart with a foot between rows.

923 *Is it completely hardy?*

It is reasonably so, but in cold areas cover with cloches in wintry spells.

924 *What sort of fertiliser does spinach require?*

Both kinds succeed on any ordinary, well-limed soil but benefit from bonemeal forked into the ground in winter. Give superphosphate, fishmeal or bonemeal at about 3 oz per sq yd on sowing and in spring. Liquid manure is helpful at times through the growing season.

925 *How can I prevent my summer spinach from bolting?*

This is probably due to over-dry conditions or poor soil or both. The secret is to keep the plants growing vigorously.

926 *I have a very light soil and find it difficult to grow spinach. Is there any special variety I might try?*

Try the rather different plant called New Zealand spinach. This is resistant to dry weather and makes a low, spreading plant. It is not fully hardy and is best started in April in a frame warmed to at least 13°C (55°F). Prick seedlings out 3 in apart in boxes and harden them off in May. They can be planted out later in the month a yard apart.

927 *Is it possible to grow this variety without using glass?*

Only in warm areas. Sow outdoors in May.

928 *When picking spinach, should I pull the whole plant or just the outer leaves?*

Summer spinach is picked regularly, as much as you like. From winter spinach take only the outer leaves. Never remove the heart of the plant until it is to be cleared away completely.

929 *What is the method for growing perpetual spinach?*

This is really a beet and is sown at almost any part of the year from March on, for summer and autumn use. It is most valuable sown in August, for winter and early spring pulling.

930 *What seeding method is needed?*

Put seed in 1½ in deep in drills 1½ ft apart, thinning the seedlings to about a foot apart.

931 *How is it harvested?*

Pulling the leaves as required. Pulling increases fresh growth.

Swedes
932 *Is it a good plan to grow swedes?*

Many people prefer turnips but swedes are larger. They are treated in much the same way as turnips and take the same amount of space. If you want to have a go, sow them in April or May, in drills a foot apart, thinning the seedlings later to 9 in.

933 *What is the secret of growing good swedes?*

Keep them well moistened through all dry spells. Dry, sandy soils tend to encourage brown heart, a disease discolouring the roots.

934 *When will they be ready?*

From September through into autumn, when the roots can be lifted and stored in a clamp like potatoes.

935 *Will they need any fresh manure?*

No, they are best grown in ground manured the previous season. Fresh manure may make roots develop irregularly.

Sweet Corn
936 *Is it possible to grow sweet corn in this country?*

It is possible, though it does best where there are long, sunny summers. It needs quite a rich soil and full sun.

937 *Is it grown from seed?*

Yes; sow at the very beginning of May, putting the seeds in small groups spaced 15 in apart in rows 3 ft apart. After germination, remove all but the strongest plants.

938 *In areas with less sunshine can I get better results by starting seeds off earlier?*

You can start seeds during mid-April in pots or boxes under glass. You need a temperature of at least 13°C (55°F). These

will then be ready for putting out towards the end of May.
You will gain a week or two by this method.

939 *Why is sweet corn sometimes grown in squares rather
than rows?*

Sweet corn must be pollinated. The male flowers hang in thin
tassels from the top of the plant and the pollen is blown on to
the lower, female flowers. Groups instead of rows increase
the chances of the pollen finding its way.

940 *Apart from normally fertile soil, does it need any special
feeding?*

You can give a general fertiliser in June or early July. It's
more important to water well. It is essential to keep the
plants growing if the weather turns dry.

941 *Suckers sometimes spring from the base of my sweet corn
plants; should these be left on or removed?*

Clear them away, leaving just the main stem.

942 *How do I know when the cobs are ripe?*

Take off an ear of corn and squeeze it. When ready, a drop
of milky juice is given off. The male tassels will be just turning brown.

943 *Sweet corn seems to take a lot of space; can I interplant
with anything else?*

You can alternate rows or patches of sweet corn with tomato
plants. Incidentally, plants grown in squares instead of rows
may be spaced more closely together, down to 15 in apart in
all directions. This also helps to keep down weeds.

944 *Is sweet corn subject to disease or pests?*

Very few, and none are likely to be a trouble.

Tarragon
945 *Is tarragon grown from seed?*

It is usual to buy small roots which are quite cheap, and put
them in during March. Large plants can be divided at the
same time. Leave a foot between plants and 18 in between
148

rows. This herb has a slightly anise flavour. and is used in stuffings or with salads.

946 *Does it need fertiliser?*

Give a top dressing of natural manure or good compost if possible, well rotted down. Repeat this each year in autumn at the same time as the stems are cut down.

Thyme
947 *As there seem to be so many different kinds of thyme, what sort should I choose?*

Common garden thyme and lemon thyme are used for herbs, the others mainly for flowers.

948 *Can I make a permanent bed of thyme?*

It is better to make a fresh bed every 2–3 years.

949 *How are these plants produced?*

Divide mature plants in April and space them out a foot apart in each direction in a hot and dry place.

950 *Won't thyme grow from seed?*

It can be sown in March or April. You can also take short cuttings in summer.

Tomatoes
951 *Can I grow tomatoes out of doors, and still get good crops?*

Yes; naturally it is easier in the warmer parts of the country and in borders that face south.

952 *What are the best varieties for outdoors?*

There are various kinds, some quite tall, though those known as bush or dwarf tomatoes are slightly hardier and require little staking. Choose early-ripening varieties.

953 *When do I sow seed for outdoor growing?*
In March, in heat at 16°C (60°F). Use first-class potting compost in small pots. Gradually harden off through to May.

I prefer to buy sturdy plants for putting out at the beginning of June.

954 *What is the best situation?*

A southern wall, facing the sun.

955 *What type of soil is best for tomatoes?*

They prefer a medium-textured soil, not too heavy, treated with rotted manure or compost and with excellent drainage.

956 *What is the tomato's main fertilising need?*

Potash should be given in the form of sulphate or muriate of potash or as wood ashes. Muriate of potash is best dug in just before planting. 2 oz per sq yd is about right. To provide phosphate, give 4 oz of bone flour as well.

957 *Is liquid manure beneficial?*

In fact it is practically essential. Feed every week in the growing season except in very dull weather.

958 *How far apart are outdoor tomatoes planted?*

18 in, in rows 2½ ft apart and of course every plant must have its stake.

959 *Do bush varieties also need stakes?*

This is not usually necessary. They are allowed to grow several branches and are pretty well self-suporting.

960 *What is the spacing for bush tomatoes?*

Usually about 2 ft each way.

961 *Why did the tomato plants I bought for outside flag so rapidly and never make good growth?*

You may have been given plants which were intended for growing under glass. Outdoor plants must be specially ordered and 'hardened off' for outdoor cultivation.

962 *What is 'hardening off'?*

This is gradually accustoming plants which have been raised

under glass to outdoor conditions, by giving them more and more ventilation each day. Finally, they are put out into cold frames, gradually removing the frames until they can withstand all temperatures, day and night.

963 *Do newly-planted plants need any protection?*

You can certainly shield early plantings by putting drainpipes or open-ended pots over each plant. This can be discontinued near the end of May.

964 *How should I put in the plants?*

Plant about 2 in deeper than their previous depth in the pots. (The soil should come 2 in up the stem.)

965 *What about watering outdoor plants?*

This is vital. The plants do not grow well unless they receive plenty of plain water. Continue this until the blossom buds appear. By sinking large plant pots 6 in from each plant and filling these with water frequently, you can ensure that the roots never dry out.

966 *Should I continue to water a lot when the fruit appears?*

Reduce the supply a little, except in severe drought. In very dry weather a surface dressing of peat, decayed compost or manure is helpful to preserve water. Keep this moistened.

967 *How can I stop the tomatoes branching?*

This applies to the tall sorts, not the bushes. At the joint of every leaf on the main stem, you will see tiny side shoots developing. Rub these off to leave just the single, vertical main stem.

968 *Presumably I do not pinch out flowering side shoots?*

Quite right, these must certainly be left! As soon as the third spray of flowers appears (fourth in favoured positions), pinch out the upward-growing tip so that the plant ceases to grow. This is usually at about 3 ft high.

969 *The bottom truss of my tomatoes nearly always fails to set fruit. Can I correct this?*

This is common outdoors and indoors and is due to ineffective natural pollination. You can buy hormone 'setting liquids' which are sprayed over the open flowers, squirting upwards into the blossoms.

970 *Will the tomatoes be normal if I do this?*

They will not contain seeds but the taste and vitamin content are the same.

971 *When should I start giving liquid manure?*

As the first fruits set.

972 *Why is it that many of the tomatoes I grow split down the side?*

The cause is probably irregular watering, particularly after very dry weather. It is better not to flood ground that has been allowed to dry out completely. Increase its moisture content gradually.

973 *Is it true that splitting can be reduced by half cutting through the main stem near the base?*

Yes; this slows the development of the plant and the flow of sap and so reduces the tendency to burst.

974 *Can I use the black polythene sheet method as with potatoes to keep weeds from soil underneath tomatoes?*

Yes, cut holes for the plants and insert them through. This method is very useful on light soil which tends to dry out very quickly. It is not so good on heavy clay, as it may encourage damp conditions favouring fungus attack.

975 *Can tomatoes be grown by the well-known 'ring culture' outdoors?*

Yes; take out a trench and lay in 5 in of moist, sandy gravel. Then stand the bottomless rings of whale-hide on this, filling them with John Innes No 1 potting compost. (You can buy this ready prepared at seed shops.) The roots will spread down from the rings into the gravel, seeking water.

976 *Using ring culture, where should I apply the water and liquid feeds?*

Pour through the compost in the rings until you are sure the roots have gone down to the gravel aggregate. After that, water the gravel and feed the compost weekly.

977 *How can I protect tomatoes against cool winds without also shielding them from the light?*

Set cloches on edge to the north of the plants.

978 *How soon can I pick tomatoes?*

As soon as they start to colour at all, it is best to take them off. This helps the remaining fruit to develop more quickly and those picked soon ripen fully.

979 *What about the green tomatoes left at the end of the season?*

These too ripen after picking off so remove them before the frosts come.

980 *Should picked green tomatoes be on a window-sill or in the dark to ripen?*

They do ripen in a dark place provided that it is warm. If you do ripen them on window-sills, remember that the tomatoes must not touch the glass, as this damages them.

981 *Is my friend right who told me always to put a few ripe fruits with unripe ones when they are being put out for ripening?*

Yes; ripe fruits give off a gas which speeds up the ripening process.

982 *How warm should ripening tomatoes be when in store?*

At least 10°C (50°F) up to 22°C (70°F). Do not let them touch each other, even if the separation is only a slip of paper.

983 *Can I grow tomatoes under cloches?*

Yes; put out seedlings in June. As the fruit ripens the plants can be pushed over to lie horizontally along the ground on clean straw or polythene sheet. Rest the cloches over them again to help in ripening.

984 *As my cloches are not high enough to accommodate tomatoes satisfactorily, can I grow them in a trench?*

To do this, dig a trench 8 in deep for extra headroom. Of course the soil below must be cultivated that little bit deeper also, and you can use the opportunity to mix in plenty of compost and phosphate fertiliser.

985 *Is it a good plan to lean plants over?*

This can also be done to give extra stem length. Tilt maturing plants to 45° and tie them carefully to angled canes.

986 *What are tomato cloches?*

These are simply ordinary tall cloches from which one side can be removed allowing the plants much better ventilation.

987 *What are the black, rotten patches on the leaves and fruit of my tomatoes?*

This is certainly blight. Prevent this by spraying at the first signs, or even before as a preventive measure, using a copper-based fungicide or Bordeaux mixture. Burn all badly infected plants.

988 *Why do some people always spray with Bordeaux mixture just before gathering the green tomatoes at the end of the year?*

This prevents blight which may develop after the tomatoes are picked for ripening.

Turnips
989 *Are turnips easy to grow?*

Yes, they develop rapidly and are also useful as catch crops between slower-growing vegetables.

990 *What is their place in crop rotation?*

The turnip is a brassica, so is grouped with cabbage, cauliflower, etc.

991 *Can I get turnips all year round?*

Almost, by sowing under cloches in February and outdoors in

March, April and May. Later, sow winter varieties in July and the first week of August. In winter, the roots need covering with leaves or straw until they are lifted.

992 *What sowing method is used?*

Fine the soil down well by raking and treading and sow the seed $\frac{1}{2}$ in deep, in rows a foot apart. The seed goes a long way. 1 oz should sow 60–80 yd. Shade summer sowings from hot sun. Thin the seedlings to about 6 in apart, but do not transplant them since this may cause bolting.

993 *What type of soil is best?*

A medium to light soil gives quickest results but turnips do reasonably well in most places.

994 *Do turnips need lime and fertilisers?*

The soil should never be acid, so apply lime at 4 oz per sq yd. 2 weeks before sowing give 4 oz per sq yd of general fertiliser, such as 1 part of sulphate of ammonia, 2 parts of sulphate of potash and 4 parts of superphosphate.

995 *How long do turnips take to mature?*

You can often start lifting small ones only 6–8 weeks after sowing.

996 *What are the pests of turnips?*

The seedlings are often attacked by flea beetle, but this can be controlled by insect sprays at and a week after sowing. Since turnip is a brassica like the cabbage, it suffers from the same problems, gall weevils, club root, etc.

997 *How big should turnips be before harvesting?*

Since they are so swift and easy to grow, it is best to lift them when they are only 3–4 in across. Incidentally, the seedlings must be thinned apart as early as possible because of this quick growth.

998 *Is it true that you can use the tops of turnips as vegetables?*

It is possible to sow turnips solely for the tops in early September, picking the leaves as they mature instead of thinning the plants in the usual way.

999 *How can stored turnips be used to grow winter salads?*

Cut the crowns from the stored turnips about $\frac{1}{2}$ in thick. Place these crown upwards on compost in a seed box. Cover, but do not bury them. Make sure though that they are pressed tightly into the soil. Finally cover them with another seedbox to keep them dark. In a warm place they will sprout fresh green leaves which can be picked off.

Watercress
1000 *Is it possible to grow watercress at home?*

Watercress requires constant supplies of fresh water and unless you have got a running stream it is not a proposition for an amateur gardener.

1001 *As I have got a stream, how do I start watercress off?*

Arrange a length of the stream to be 2 or 3 in deep and simply poke in rooted pieces of watercress 3 in apart over the stream bottom. If they tend to loosen hold them down with stones temporarily. They will soon establish themselves and give you good salad picking with very little trouble.

Table of Imperial and Metric Measures

Length

1 in	=	2.5 cm
3 in	=	7.6 cm
6 in	=	15.2 cm
9 in	=	22.8 cm
12 in = 1 ft	=	30.5 cm
3 ft = 1 yd	=	0.9 m
2 yd	=	1.8 m

Weight

1 oz	=	28.4 g
1 lb	=	450 g
1 cwt	=	51 kg

Capacity

1 pt	=	570 ml
2 pt = 1 quart	=	1.14 l
8 pt = 1 gal	=	4.5 l

Area

1 sq ft	=	930 sq cm
1 sq yd	=	8400 sq cm

Also available in Sphere Books

ARABELLA BOXER'S GARDEN COOKBOOK
Arabella Boxer

In this imaginative yet really practical book, Arabella Boxer presents over 300 recipes varying from the exotic right down to unusual ways to prepare the simple potato. Her aim is to enable the cook not only to recognize the nutritional value of vegetables, but also to enjoy their infinite variety. The book is also a comprehensive reference book, including every vegetable and herb from agar-agar and Brussels sprouts to zucchini.

0 7221 1798 1   95p

THE KITCHEN GARDEN
Keith Mossman

Keith Mossman draws upon a lifetime's experience to show how even the smallest town garden, indoors or out, can yield a variety of organically grown foods which are cheaper, healthier and tastier than the products from the local supermarket. With this book everyone can fight the war against artificial foods and escalating prices by growing their own fresh food – in pots and tubs, on window sills and patios, on small plots of land and on roof gardens.

0 7221 6252 9   65p

All Sphere Books are available at your bookshop or newsagent, or can be ordered from the following address: Sphere Books, Cash Sales Department, P.O. Box 11, Falmouth, Cornwall.

Please send cheque or postal order (no currency), and allow 19p for postage and packing for the first book plus 9p per copy for each additional book ordered up to a maximum charge of 73p in U.K.

Customers in Eire and B.F.P.O. please allow 19p for postage and packing for the first book plus 9p per copy for the next 6 books, thereafter 3p per book.

Overseas customers please allow 20p for postage and packing for the first book and 10p per copy for each additional book.